T0330818

The Selection and Use of Contract Research Organizations

The Selection and Use of Contract Research Organizations

A guide for the pharmaceutical and medical device industries

Shayne C. Gad

Taylor & Francis
Taylor & Francis Group

LONDON AND NEW YORK

First published 2003 by Taylor & Francis
11 New Fetter Lane, London EC4P 4EE

Simultaneously published in the USA and Canada
by Taylor & Francis Inc,
29 West 35th Street, New York, NY 10001

Taylor & Francis is an imprint of the Taylor & Francis Group

© 2003 Taylor & Francis

Typeset in 9/14pt Stone Serif by Graphicraft Limited, Hong Kong
Printed and bound in Great Britain by Antony Rowe Ltd, Chippenham, Wiltshire

All rights reserved. No part of this book may be reprinted or reproduced or utilised in any form
or by any electronic, mechanical, or other means, now known or hereafter invented, including
photocopying and recording, or in any information storage or retrieval system, without permission
in writing from the publishers.

Every effort has been made to ensure that the advice and information in this book is true and
accurate at the time of going to press. However, neither the publisher nor the authors can accept
any legal responsibility or liability for any errors or omissions that may be made. In the case of drug
administration, any medical procedure or the use of technical equipment mentioned within this
book, you are strongly advised to consult the manufacturer's guidelines.

British Library Cataloguing in Publication Data
A catalogue record for this book is available from the British Library

Library of Congress Cataloging in Publication Data
A catalogue record has been requested

ISBN 0-415-29903-9

Dedication

To Carrol S. Weil, my first boss and a model for what a contract laboratory scientist can become. We all miss you.

Shayne C. Gad

Contents

Preface

I was privileged to start my career in toxicology more than 25 years ago in a testing laboratory that was a hybrid of a company lab and a contract testing lab. The Chemical Hygiene Fellowship of Carnegie Mellon Institute of Research (later known as Bushy Run Labs) was a near perfect environment to learn the practical aspects of regulatory toxicology testing while also being pushed to stay abreast of the then rapidly flowering science of toxicology. Though I have not worked in the contract research environment full time since then, the insights, work ethic and friendships from those days have been invaluable.

At least through the point of completion of initial studies in humans, most pharmaceutical and medical device development is performed by one form or another of contractor. It is only because of contract research organizations (CROs) that recent advances in basic science have been translated to the medical wonders that have become available the last ten years, with the CROs providing the essential regulatory compliant underpinnings of science and technology. Success in pharmaceutical and medical device development requires many things, but the probability of a positive outcome is vastly improved if the individuals and companies seeking to develop these new products truly understand the 'tools' before them. Improving that understanding is the objective of this book.

Introduction

The research driven components of the global health care industry represent an enormous economic and societal force in the world, and are composed of an incredibly diverse set of component organizations. Ranging from huge multinational corporations to 'virtual' organizations which have only a few part time employees, while primarily in the private sector, there are also those which are partially or fully funded by various government organizations (there is probably even room for a separate volume on funding models and means for such organizations and the impact of such on development processes). There are 'for pay' directories of these available (DIA, 2002 for example), but these are by no means either comprehensive of objective.

For the purposes of this volume, the resulting products from all of the efforts of this sector of the global economy include drugs (pharmaceuticals, biologicals, vaccines and so forth), medical devices, and diagnostics. All of these are highly regulated both during their development and marketing. Though many of the service organizations referred to in this volume also do work for other industries, our focus will be on the more limited pharmaceutical and medical device industrial sector.

Contract research organizations (CROs) (also called CSOs – contract service organizations, or PDOs – pharmaceutical development organizations) span an amazing range of areas of expertise. Though there are some organizations which present themselves as turn-key 'we do it all' (none timely do), most offer distinct niche services. These include:

1 *Biological*: Pharmacology (*in vitro* screening, efficacy modeling, safety pharmacology), toxicology (genetic toxicology, animal toxicology – with many subsets), pharmacokinetics and metabolism.
2 *Chemistry*: Synthesis, active pharmaceutical ingredient (API) manufacture, radiolabeled synthesis, analytical methods, bioanalytical methods.
3 *Clinical*: Phase I centers, clinical research associates (CRA), statisticians, data and site management, report writing services. Centerwatch.com currently lists more than 730 of these for the US alone.

4 *Dosage form aspects*: Formulation developers, clinical test material (CTM) manufacturers (oral, topical and parenteral), labeling, patient kit preparation.

5 *Regulatory*: Investigative new drug (IND) applications, new drug applications (NDA), and annual update writers, regulatory advisors.

A more detailed breakdown of the scope and types of activities of CROs is provided in Chapter 4. Literally the services provided cover the entire range of activities involved in discovering, developing, getting market approval for manufacturing, distributing and marketing the products in these industries. I will limit this volume to those involved in taking an idea or molecule forward through development to the point of getting regulatory approval to market a product.

I must also state that most of my career has been spent in the aspects involved in insuring the safety of products, and therefore I will tend to use the CROs ('toxicology labs') and activities in this area as examples. While such have been the subject of limited directories in the past (Jackson, 1985; Texas Research Institute, 1986 and Freudenthal, 1997), they have been limited to larger US facilities.

We should start by considering the history of such commercial labs. The oldest in the US (Food and Drug Research Laboratories or FDRL) opened in the 1930s, moved from suburban New Jersey to rural upstate New York, and went out of operation in the late 1980s, though the facilities are still utilized by (and some of the staff still work at) Liberty Laboratories, which specializes in felines (domestic cats) for and in research.

From the second half of the 1970s a number of toxicology laboratories [Industrial Biotest (IBT), the University of Miami operated lab, Cannon Laboratories, Bioassay Systems, Lilton Biometrics, Tegaris Labs, Bushy Run (for years called the Chemical Hygiene Fellowship of Carnegie Mellon Institute and perhaps the second oldest contract toxicology laboratory), Borriston/Midatlantic Laboratories, Primate Research Institute (PRI), Utah Biomedical Testing Laboratory (UBTL), HTI, and Oread Laboratories – to name a few] of significant size have gone out of existence. Additionally, just as in the industries they serve, there has been a continued series of acquisitions and mergers (the current Charles River Laboratories includes what were once Sierra Biomedical, Pathology Associates Incorporated, Argus Research, Redfield Laboratory, Springborn Laboratories and TSI Mason among its parts) and of renamings (Hazleton becoming Corning becoming Covance, for example). These same trends and forces have been active in the other types of CROs. As has continued shifting (and generally) expansion of services offered to expand market, revenues and profitability. In extreme cases this has led to the evolution of some organizations (such as Quintiles, Covance, and MDS Pharma) which offer to 'do it all' for the pharmaceutical industry.

Few companies seeking to develop a new regulated product (though the focus of this book is on drugs, devices and diagnostics, this also applies to dietary supplements, pesticides, cosmetics and many other products) have the capability to perform the required technical (and in many cases, regulatory) work needed to bring the product to market. From this point such companies will be generally referred to as clients or sponsors. Alternatively, although some or all of the capabilities may exist, the company's laboratory schedule may not be able to accommodate all required works in the desired time frame. At some time, for various reasons, industry will need to contract work to external facilities, whether they are commercial contract laboratories, university laboratories, or even a member company's laboratory as in the case of a consortium study. As with all contractual arrangements, careful planning and coordination coupled with thorough preparation is required in order to obtain the desired product or service, to avoid confusion and misunderstanding, and to produce a timely and cost effective result. This is a practical guide for those organizations that need to outsource some or all of their activities at external facilities. Here I shall attempt to present both the how of such activities and a source book (directory) of those that are available.

The needs for (and means of accessing) CRO support services are different for the majority of client organizations (smaller companies which have no or only one marketed product) and larger organizations (sometimes referred to as 'big pharma', comprising truly fully integrated companies with multiple products on the market). Issues of timing, cash flow and objective (get the product to a point where a 'partner' will buy or at least heavily support the continued development of a product versus taking products all the way to market) as well as what contract resources are needed and how they are to be managed as part of a development program tend to be very different. But the majority of the concerns and issues of individual contractory selection, monitoring, and management as presented in this book are common (FDA, 1984).

DEFINING THE PROJECT

Development of the study record

The objective of a study or any research is to evaluate theories and produce results. The written record of this work is called the study record and includes all records, documentation, and results of the development effort. Let us now consider the logical progression of such research activities and the development of the study record.

Research plan

The development project begins with developing the study or project plan, or simply thinking through what needs to be done and when. Whether the worker is performing internal research, concept evaluations, or works in support of regulatory requirements, this plan should be written down. When written, the research plan becomes the framework for the protocol or contract for the project and includes the hypothesis, the proposed methods, observations to be made, and the expected results. Researchers should pay special attention to the level of detail in this plan. For example, in regulatory research environments there are mandated requirements for inclusion of particular details in the protocol and a specified format. Optional experimental methods may be included in the protocol or amended into it as needed, but (again) must be recorded. Even if a written protocol or detailed contract is not specifically required for the project, it is useful to develop the habit of producing a protocol because it requires you and your colleagues to think clearly through the experimental design and potential issues. It also provides guidance for the actual conduct of the work and promotes consistency in performance (Figure 1.1).

General considerations

There are a number of general aspects to be considered in the operations of a CRO in the regulated industries that we are concerned with. Most of these, of course, have to do with how things are documented. I will generally use US FDA Good Laboratory Practices (GLPs) (FDA, 2002c) as my model in this volume, but the principles are the same internationally (Gad, 2001) and for Good Manufacturing Practices (GMPs) and Good Clinical Practices (GCPs).

```
┌─────────────────────────────────────────────┐
│           Research Plan or Protocol           │
│                      ↓                        │
│      Standard Operation Procedures (SOPs)     │
│                      ↓                        │
│   Recording Observations – Data Generation    │
│                      ↓                        │
│              Evaluation of Data               │
│                      ↓                        │
│     Report of Data, Results and Conclusion    │
│                      ↓                        │
│          Report Review and Revision           │
│                      ↓                        │
│             Final Report Issuance             │
└─────────────────────────────────────────────┘
```

Figure 1.1: Progression of a contracted study or project.

Standard operating procedures

Some of the procedures performed during the study are routine for the laboratory. Formalize the documentation of these routine procedures into written standard operating procedures (SOPs). SOPs are detailed descriptions of such things as equipment operation, methods for taking and recording data, and procedures for reagent receipt, storage, and preparation – the types of procedures that are common to all laboratory operations. Write SOPs in sufficient detail to promote consistency in performing the procedures. Having SOPs and insisting that they are followed provides the researcher with a measure of control over potential variables in the experiment.

A good place to initiate an evaluation of any regulated facility is to examine its record of previous inspection results. For the FDA, these are easy to obtain (FDA, 2002b).

Data recording

The study begins. You perform a procedure, write down what you did, and record the observed results. The level of detail of any written record should enable someone else with equivalent technical training to perform your experiment exactly as you did. Why? *Reproducibility.* That experimental results must be reproducible is a basic rule of science. It is the process through which scientific conclusions and discoveries are confirmed. Reproducibility is promoted by the specific data-recording requirements for data that are submitted to the FDA and equivalent non-US regulatory agencies. Reproducibility is also required in research performed to support a patent request.

■ 5

For now, I wish to introduce you to the concept of 'if you didn't write it down you didn't do it'. You, the researcher, have the burden of proof in regulated research, in protection of patent rights, and in defense of your work in professional circles. The issue is *completeness* of your records. The study record must be a complete record of all data and procedures performed. If you didn't write it down, you didn't do it. In the experimental record, there are some accepted shortcuts. Here some of the hard preparatory work pays off. In your written record, you may include references to previously described methods and SOPs, state that they were followed exactly, or describe deviations from them. And efficient ways of collecting data may be developed to encourage the complete recording of all required data. Later in this chapter, methods for recording procedures and observations will be discussed in detail.

The *accuracy* of recorded data is another important consideration because any observed result, if not recorded immediately, may not be record accurately. Don't lose data because of some rationalization about time, money, or your ability to remember what happened. All data should be recorded directly into a notebook or onto a worksheet at the time of the observation. Also, transcribed data – data copied by hand or entered by a person into a computer – often is subject to errors. If data are copied to a table or a spreadsheet, the entered data should be checked against the original data to ensure accuracy. In a regulated research work, all such work and data will also be audited and the accuracy and conformance to procedure verified.

Analysis of the data

When the laboratory work is done, the analysis of the data begins. Observed data are entered into formulas, calculations are made, and statistical analysis is performed. All these manipulations must be carefully recorded, for from these data the conclusions will be drawn. The manipulations of the data are the link between the original observation and the conclusions. Consistency between the data and the result is controlled by monitoring all transcription, manipulation, and correlations of the data in generation of the final manuscript.

Reporting of results and conclusions

Finally, the draft final report is provided for review, to the client and/or their agent. It will receive critical review before acceptance. The final version will then be provided to others and again will receive critical review by other scientists or some skeptical governmental or public audience. In all cases, it will be essential to be able to justify the data. The methods, initial data, the calculations and statistical analysis, and the conclusions must be defensible, meaning complete, accurate, internally consistent, and repeatable to withstand scientific criticism.

TYPES OF DATA

Earlier I mentioned different elements of the study record: research plan or protocol, observations, calculations and statistical output, and conclusions. For ease of explanation, the terminology from the GLPs, GMPs and GCPs (from here on GLPs will be used to stand for all three in the general case) – protocol, raw data, statistical analysis, and final report – will be used to describe the components of the study record.

From the GLPs, the protocol is a written document that is approved by the study director (person responsible for the technical conduct of the study) and sponsoring organization. The protocol is the research plan, or the project plan in a management sense. It clearly indicates the objectives of the research project and describes all methods for the conduct of the work. It includes a complete description of the test system, the text article, the experimental design, the data to be collected, the type and frequency of tests, and planned statistical analysis.

The protocol will be strictly followed during research. 'What', you say, 'no experimental license, no free expression of scientific inquiry?' Of course there is, as long as the changes in procedures or methods are documented. If the work you are doing is governed by strict contractual or regulatory guidelines, you may not be able to express much creativity, but remember, the objective, in this case, is to provide consistent and reliable comparisons for regulatory purposes. Even the GLPs make provisions to amend the protocol and document deviations from it. During all research, except perhaps during the most routine analysis, there may be changes in experimental methods and procedures, rethinking of design, decisions to analyze data in new or different ways, or unexpected occurrences that cause mistakes to be made. An important concept to apply here is that these variances from the plan must be documented.

Raw data

'Raw data' is the term used to describe the most basic element of experimental observations. It is important to understand fully the concept of raw data.

There are unique standards for recording raw data that do not apply to other types of data. These will be discussed later in the chapter. For now, let us look at what constitutes raw data. In the FDA and Environmental Protection Agency (EPA) GLPs,

> *. . . raw data means any laboratory worksheets, records, memoranda, notes or exact copies thereof that are the result of original observation and activities of the study and are necessary for the reconstruction and evaluation of the report of that study.*

All terms must be taken in the most literal sense and must be interpreted collectively to apply this definition to the data generated during an experiment. There are two key phrases: 'are the result of original observations and activities of the study', and 'are necessary for the reconstruction and evaluation of the report of that study'. Raw data include visual observations, measurements, output of instrumental measurements, and any activity that describes or has an impact on the observations. Anything that is produced or observed during the study that is necessary to reconstruct (know what happened) and evaluate (analyze or, for regulatory purposes, assess the quality of) the reported results and conclusions is raw data. This definition of raw data has been carefully designed to encourage the development of data that are defensible.

Included in the scope of raw data may be data that result from calculations that allow the data to be analyzed, for example, the results of gas chromatography where the raw data are defined as the curve that was fitted by the instrument software from individual points. The individual points on the curve are essentially meaningless by themselves, but the curve provides the needed basic information. The area under the curve, which is used to calculate the concentration, is an interpretation of the curve based on decisions made about the position of the baseline and the height of the peak. This is not 'raw data' since it is not the original observation and may be calculated later and, practically, may be recalculated. For the researcher to understand the results completely, the curve with the baseline, the area under the curve, and the calculations are required and recorded, but only the curve itself is 'raw data.' The distinction is that the curve is the original observation and must be recorded promptly. The current advance of 'section' of the GLPs, governing how electronic (automated data are collected, manipulated, audited, verified, stored and provided to the FDA) adds another entire dimension to consideration of there issues.

Other types of data

Other types of data that are not thought of as raw data may be included here. For example, correspondence, memoranda, and notes that may include information that is necessary to reconstruct and evaluate the reported results and conclusions. While these are not records of original experimental observations, they do represent documentation of the activities of the study. They often contain approvals for method changes by study management or sponsoring organizations, instructions to laboratory staff for performing procedures, or ideas recorded during the work. Here are some examples of raw data that are generated during a toxicology study:

Test article receipt documents	Equipment use and calibration
Animal receipt documents	Equipment maintenance
Records of quarantine	Transfer of sample custody
Dose formulation records	Sample randomization
Sample collection records	Animal or sample identification
Dosing records	Assignment to study
Animal observations	Necropsy records
Blood collections and analysis	Analytical results
Euthanasia records	Histology records
Pathologist's findings	

For government-regulated research, all records that are documentation of the study conduct are treated as raw data. From the perspective of the scientific historian, the original notes, correspondence, and observations tell the story of the life and thought processes of the scientist being studied. From the mundane to the extreme, these records are important.

Computerized data collection

Special attention must be dedicated to computer-generated raw data. Automated laboratory instrumentation has come into widespread use. In hand-recorded data, the record of the original observation is raw data. But what is considered raw data in computerized systems? In this case, raw data are the first recorded occurrence of the original observation that is human readable. This definition treats computer-generated data as hand-recorded data. It documents the 'original observations and activities of the study and is necessary for reconstruction and evaluation of the report of that study' (FDA, 1987; EPA,

1989a, b). However, we must pay special attention to this type of data. The validity of hand-recorded data is based on the reliability of the observer and on well-developed and validated standards of measurement. For computer-generated data, the observer is a computerized data collection system, and the measurements are controlled by a computer program. These are complex systems that may contain complex flaws. Just as the principles behind measurements with a standard thermometer were validated centuries ago and are verified with each thermometer produced today, so must modern computerized instrumentation be validated and its operation verified. This causes a real dilemma for many scientists who are proficient in biomedical research but not in computer science. Because of the size and scope of this issue, I can only call your attention to the problem and refer you to the literature for additional guidance. Finally moving to promulgation and clarification of requirements of GLP section 11 (21 CFR 11; FDA 1997a, b) compliance, though it is still not completely clear all that will be required, seven elements are involved: software validation, logon security, audit trails, authority controls (over entries and changes), storage of data, backup and archives, and training for users and administration.

Statistical data

Statistical data result from descriptive processes, summarization of raw data, and statistical analysis. Simply put, these data are not raw data but represent manipulation of the data. However, during this analysis process, a number of situations may affect the raw data and the final conclusions. For example, certain data may be rejected because they are shown to be experimentally flawed, an outlier believed to have resulted from an error, or not plausible. I will leave it to other texts to discuss the criteria by which decisions like these are made. Here, I will say only that any manipulation of raw data is itself raw data. For example, a series of organ weights is analyzed. One of the weights is clearly out of the usual range for the species, and no necropsy observations indicated the organ was of unusual size. The preserved tissues are checked, and the organ appears to be the same size as others in the group. The statistician then may decide to remove that organ weight from the set of weights. This record of this action is raw data. The analysis is not, because it can be replicated. It is a fine distinction that matters only in the context of recording requirements for raw data since both the analyses and record of the data change are required to reconstruct the report.

Statistical analysis is part of the study record. Documentation of the methods of statistical analysis, statistical parameters, and calculations is important. Critical evaluation of conclusions often involves discussion of the statistical methods employed. Complete documentation and reporting of these methods, calculations, and results allows for constructive, useful critical review.

Results and conclusions

The study record includes the results and conclusions made from review of the data produced during the scientific investigation. The data are summarized in abstracts, presented at meetings, published in journals, and, with all previously discussed types of data, are reported to government agencies. However, it is the scientist's interpretation of the data that communicates the significance of the experimentation. In all scientific forums, scientists present their interpretation of the data as results and conclusions. Results and conclusions are separate concepts. This is an important distinction not only because it is the required format for journal articles and reports, but because it is important to separate them in one's understanding. Results are a literal, objective description of the observations made during the study, a statement of the facts. Conclusions, on the other hand, represent the analysis of the significance of these observations. They state the researcher's interpretation of the results. If results are presented clearly and objectively, they can be analyzed by any knowledgeable scientist, thereby testing the conclusions drawn. This is the process by which the body of scientific knowledge is refined and perfected.

For regulatory purposes, the results presented to the regulatory agencies (FDA or equivalent) must be complete. Included in the reports submitted are tables of raw data, all factors that affect the data, and summaries of the data. In journals, the results section usually is a discussion with tabular or graphical presentations of what the researcher considers relevant data to support the conclusions. Conclusions presented in either case interpret the data, discuss the significance of the data, and describe the rationale for reaching the stated conclusions. In both bases, the results are reviewed and the conclusions analyzed by scientific peers. The function of the peer review process is to question and dispute or confirm the information gained from the experiment. Objective reporting of results and clear discussion of conclusions are required to communicate the scientist's perspective successfully to the scientific community.

DEVELOPMENT OF STUDY DATA

Above we have discussed the types of data that make up the study record. The following discussion addresses: quality characteristics for the study record, requirements for recording raw data, and methods for fulfilling the quality characteristics and raw data requirements by using various record-keeping formats.

Quality characteristics

There are four characteristics the study record must have: completeness, consistency, accuracy, and reconstructability. *Completeness* means the information is totally there, self-explanatory, and whole. *Consistency* in the study record means that there is 'reasonable agreement between different records containing the same information' (DeWoskin, 1995). *Accuracy* is agreement between what is observed and what is recorded. The final characteristic is *reconstructability*. Can the data record guide the researcher or someone else through the events of the study? These characteristics are goals to meet in developing the study record and will be used in Chapter 4 to evaluate the quality of these records. They must be built into the study from the beginning, and considerable attention to these goals will be required as the study progresses to produce a complete, consistent, accurate, and reconstructable study record.

Recording raw data

Raw data may be recorded by hand in laboratory notebooks and worksheets or entered into a computerized data management system. Today, more and more data are computer generated and recorded as paper outputs or are electronically written to magnetic media, microfiche, or other storage media. This section will discuss how raw data in both forms are recorded.

General requirements for raw data recording

Raw data must be recorded properly to preserve and protect them. The following is an excerpt from the FDA GLPs:

> *All data generated during the conduct of a study, except those*
> *that are generated by automated data collection systems, shall*

*be recorded **directly, promptly, and legibly in ink**. All data entries shall be **dated on the date of entry** and **signed or initialed by the person entering the data**. [Emphasis added.]*

All introductory laboratory courses teach these basic techniques for recording raw data. Even though these standards are published as regulations for only certain types of research, I believe that there is never an instance when these minimum standards do not apply. There may be researchers who 'get by' writing in pencil or scribbling data on paper towels, but they often suffer the consequences of their carelessness when data are lost or their records are unintelligible. Furthermore, if these same researchers attempt to patent a product or method, or to submit their data to regulatory agencies, their data are not acceptable. In fact, if the regulatory data are incomplete or obscured in some way, the scientist involved may be subject to civil or criminal penalties. It is always best to establish good habits early, especially for scientific record keeping.

For hand-recorded data, 'directly, promptly, and legibly in ink' means to write it down in the notebook or on the worksheet as soon as you see it, so it is readable and in ink. The purpose is to preserve accurately the observation. Notes on paper towels or scraps of paper may be lost. Prompt recording promotes accuracy. Legibility assures that later you will understand what is written. This does not necessarily mean neat. If you are recording directly and promptly, neatness may have to be forgone. It does, however, mean readable and understandable.

The use of ink preserves the record from being erased or smeared. It is commonly understood that the ink should be indelible, meaning it cannot be erased and can withstand water or solvent spills. Some organizations may require a specific color of ink to be used, usually black or dark blue. This requirement originated because black ink was the most permanent and could be photocopied. Without such requirements, the ink used in the lab should be tested to see how it withstands common spills and to see if it copies on the standard photocopier. Some colors of ink and some thin line pens may not copy completely. There are a number of reasons why data may need to be copied, and that they are copied exactly becomes a very practical issue. Inks should not fade with time. Some analytical instruments produce printed data on heat-sensitive paper. To preserve these data, laboratories will make photocopies. This is an issue that will be discussed more fully in Chapter 3.

THE SELECTION AND USE OF CROs

The requirements to sign and date the data record flow from practical and legal considerations; it is often useful to know who made and recorded the observation. In many research labs, graduate assistants or research technicians are responsible for recording the raw data. If questions arise later, the individual responsible may be sought out and asked to clarify an entry. For GLP studies, the signature represents a legal declaration meaning the data recorded here are correct and complete. The data must be dated at the time of entry. This attests to the date of the recording of the observation and the progression in time of the study conduct. Some lab work is time dependent and in this case the time and date must be recorded. There is no instance when data or signatures may be backdated or dated in advance.

Signatures and dates are crucial when documenting discovery and in supporting a patent claim. For studies conducted under the GLPs, the signature and date are legal requirements for the reconstruction of the study conduct. Falsely reported data may then result in civil or criminal penalties to the person recording the data and his/her management for making false and misleading statements.

In some types of research, additional signatures and dates may be required. Data used to support a patent and data generated during the manufacture of drugs or medical devices must be signed and dated by an additional person – a witness or reviewer thus corroborating the stated information.

Error correction in data recording

What happens when there is a mistake in recording data or an addition that must be made to the data at a later time? The FDA GLPs address this.

> *Any changes to entries shall be made so as not to obscure the original entry, shall indicate the reason for such change, and shall be dated and signed at the time of the change.*

All changes to the written record of data must be explained and signed and dated. Doing so provides justification for the correction and again provides testimony as to who made the change and when it was done. To make corrections to the data, the original entry is not obscured. A single line is drawn through the entry. Then, the reason for the change is recorded with the date the change is made and the initials of the person making the change. A code may be established and documented to explain common reasons for making corrections to data. A simple example may be a circled letter designation like:

S = sentence error

E = entry error

X = calculation error

This is easy to remember and use. Any other types of errors or corrections must be described in sufficient detail to justify the change.

Raw data may be generated by computer programs and stored on paper or magnetic medial. Most laboratories approach this kind of data as they would hand-generated data. The GLPs state:

> *In automated data collection systems, the individual respons-ible for direct data input shall be identified at the time of the data input. Any changes to automated data entries shall be made so as not to obscure the original entry, shall indicate the reason for the change, shall be dated and the responsible individual shall be identified.*

For automated data collection systems, there are similar standards to hand-recorded data (FDA, 1987). All raw data should be recorded promptly and directly. Whereas the requirement for hand-collected data is that records be written legibly and in ink, permanence and security of computer-collected data is the requirement. However, there may be special considerations for how signatures and dates are recorded. Physical signature of data may not be possible when using electronic storage media. Electronic signature or the recording of the operator's name and the date are often a function provided in the software and are recorded with the data. When the data are printed in a paper copy, this information should be included. Some labs have adopted a policy requiring that the paper printout must be signed and dated by the operator. Some instruments produce a continuous printout or strip chart. In this case, the chart should be signed by the operator and dated on the date the data are retrieved. If the data are maintained on electronic media, the operator's name and date must be recorded on that medium.

Because computer security and risk of corruption or destruction of computer-stored data are a major concern, many laboratories maintain computer-generated data in paper printouts because the means for maintain-ing the data are traditional and easy to implement. As long as the printout represents a verified exact copy of the original raw data, it is acceptable and often even preferable to designate the printout as the raw data.

When changes to the electronically stored raw data are made, the original observation must be maintained. This is accomplished in several ways. Newer software packages allow these changes to be made and properly documented. To do this, the original entry is not erased, and there is a way of recording the reason for the change along with the electronic signature of the person authorized to make the change and the date of the change. However, some data collection systems still do not have this capability. If this is the case, the original printout may be retained with the new printout that contains the change, the reason for the change, the signature of the person authorized to make the change, and the date of the change. Some computer programs allow for footnotes and addenda to be added to the record. These additions to the record, if made later, should also include a handwritten or computer-recorded signature and date.

FORMATS FOR RECORDING DATA

We will now begin to construct the study record. The format for the study record may be determined by the preferences of the researcher. Some researchers prefer to maintain all study records in laboratory notebooks. In private industry, research and development labs may be required to use lab notebooks because of potential patent documentation requirements. Many chemists have become accustomed to the use of lab notebooks. However, handwritten data may be maintained in laboratory notebooks, on worksheets and forms, or one may use computer-generated printouts and electronic storage media. The remainder of this section discusses guidelines for recording data using all formats.

Laboratory notebooks

Laboratory notebooks are usually bound books with ruled or gridded pages that are used to record the events of an experiment. Organizations may order specially prepared notebooks that are uniquely numbered on the cover and spine. They have consecutively numbered pages, and some come with additional carbonless pages to make exact copies of the entries. Organizations may have procedures in place for issuing notebooks to individuals for use on specific research projects. After the glassware is cleaned, all that remains of a study is the notebook; its value is the cost of repeating all the work. Therefore, SOPs should be written to control the assignment, use, and location of these records.

The pages may be designed to contain formats for recording information. In the header, there may be space for the title and date. In the footer, space may be allocated for signature and date of the recorder, and signature and date of a reviewer or witness. When beginning to use a laboratory notebook, set aside the first few pages for the table of contents. Then a few pages may be held in reserve for notes, explanations, and definitions that are generally applicable to the contents.

The remainder of this section discusses the rules for recording data in the notebook. First, each page should contain a descriptive title of the experiment that includes the study designation and the experimental procedure to be performed. The date the procedure was performed is also recorded. Often a complete description of the experiment will require several pages. After the first page, subsequent pages should indicate, at least, an abbreviated title and cross-reference to the page from which it was continued.

The body of the experimental record should include the following sections:

- Purpose of the experiment
- Materials needed, including instruments, equipment and reagents
- Reagent and sample preparation
- Methods and procedures
- Results

The *purpose* may be recorded in a few sentences. The *materials section* is a list of all the things you need for the experiment – the instruments to be used, the equipment, and chemicals. When recording the analytical instruments, include the make, model number, and serial number; the location of the instrument; and all settings and conditions for the use of the instrument. The description of the chemical used should include a complete description including name, manufacturer, lot or serial number, and concentration. *Reagent and solution* preparation must be described in detail with a record of all weights and measurements. It is extremely important that sample identification and sample preparation be completely documented. The *methods and procedures* section is a step-by-step description of the conduct of the experiment.

If SOPs are in place that describe any of the above information in sufficient detail, they may be referenced. Then information recorded in the notebook is all weights and measurements, and any information that is unique to this experiment or not specifically discussed in the SOP. SOPs often are written for more general applications. An SOP may state that the pH will be adjusted using a buffer or acid as required. The notebook should indicate what was used to adjust the pH and how much was used. An SOP may describe the formulation of a compound in a certain amount, when the experiment requires a different amount. The mixing procedures may be cross-referenced, but it will be necessary to describe in detail the conversion of the SOP quantities and any changes in procedure resulting from the change in quantity.

The *experimental results* section must contain all observations and any information relating to those results. It should include any deviation from established methods, from SOPs, and from the protocol. Failed experiments must be reported even though the procedure was successfully repeated. Justification for repeating the procedure and a description of what may have gone wrong is recorded. All calculations should include a description of the formula used.

Remember, all entries are recorded directly and promptly into the notebook at the time of the experiment and are recorded legibly in ink. Some information may be entered at the beginning of the day, some entered at the end of the day, but all weights, measurements, and recorded observations must be entered into the notebook directly and promptly.

For a complete record, it is often necessary to insert such information as shipping receipts, photographs, and printouts into the lab notebook. In doing so, do not obscure any writing on the page. The following are tips for inserting information into the notebook.

- Glue the loose paper in place. (I do not recommend using tape because tape over time loses its holding power.)
- Inserts may be signed, dated, and cross-referenced to the notebook and page so that they can be replaced if they become loose.
- Make verified copies of data that are too large for the page, shrinking it to fit the notebook page.
- If, by some chance, data are accidentally recorded on a paper towel or other handy scrap of paper, these should be signed, dated, and glued into the notebook. It is not wise to transcribe data, introducing the possibility of error and the distasteful possibility of data tampering.

The bottom of each page must be signed by the person entering the data and dated at the time of entry. The date at the top of the page – the date of the activity – in most cases will be the same as the date at the bottom of the page. A few exceptions are appropriate. The most legitimate exception to this rule occurs when a page is reserved for the results printout. The printout may not be available to insert until the following day. The printout should indicate the date when the data were first recorded, which should in turn match the top date. The date at the bottom of the page indicates when it was glued into the notebook.

Occasionally, a scientist will forget to sign and date the page. When this happens, there is no quick fix. The only remedy is to add a notation: 'This page was not signed and dated on ____, the time of entry'. Then, sign and date this statement.

This discussion has been detailed because the signature and dates on the pages are very important. They are legally required for regulatory purposes. Data used to support patents and specified data produced under the FDA current Good Manufacturing Practices (GMPs) and Good Clinical Practices (GCPs) require the signature and date of a witness or reviewer. For example, the GMPs require that all materials weighed or measured in the preparation of the drug be witnessed, signed, and dated. Patent applications are supported by witnessed experimental records. Some institutions may require supervisory review of notebook entries with accompanying signature and date. This is to say that you should be aware of the uses of your data and any requirements for this additional signature.

An important concept to remember is that bound, consecutively page-numbered notebooks are used to demonstrate the progression of the research and to document the dates of data entry and when the work was performed. To prevent the corruption of this record, unused and partially used pages may be marked out so no additions may be made. A suggested method is to draw a 'Z' through the page or portion of the page not used. At the end of the project, there may be used notebook pages. These may be 'Z'd', or the last page may indicate that this is the end of the experimental record and no additional pages will be used.

Forms and worksheets

While many analytical laboratories continue to use lab notebooks, other labs may use forms and worksheets to record their data. The purpose is to provide an efficient format for recording data that are routine in nature. The basic concept is that forms and worksheets should be designed to be easy to use and to provide a complete record of all relevant data. They may be used in combination with lab notebooks as described above or kept in files or loose-leaf binders. Explanatory footnotes may be preprinted or added to explain abbreviations and/or the meaning of symbols. Additional space for comments and notes should be incorporated into the format.

Computer spreadsheets and word processing make forms and worksheets easy to design and produce.

The advantages of using forms and worksheets include the following:

- They may be formatted to prompt for all necessary information.
- They are easy to follow and complete.
- Header information, title, study designation, sample numbers, etc. may be filled out in advance, thus saving time.
- Cross-references to applicable SOPs may be included on the worksheet.
- They help to standardize data collection.

Disadvantages of using forms and worksheets include the following:

- They must be carefully designed and should be pretested for completeness and ease of use.
- They may encourage a tendency not to write more information than is specifically requested. Space should be allotted for notes and comments.
- Forms and worksheets that are designed for general use may contain blanks that are not necessary for the current study. Yet all blanks must be completed. If not needed, 'n/a' (not applicable) should be written in the blank or a dash put in the space.
- Forms and worksheets create a routine that can become mindless; take care to complete the form properly.
- Example 1: Necropsy forms often contain a complete list of tissues to be checked by the technician. When only some tissues are inspected or retrieved, it may be too easy to check (tick) inappropriate boxes.
- Example 2: Animal behavioral observation forms contain blanks to record all observations. The observer must record something in the blank space. A check or 'OK' may be used for normal behavior if defined on the form or in an SOP. A problem occurs when these designations are used automatically without proper attention to observing and recording the behavior of each animal, particularly when most animals are behaving normally.

In discussing the above disadvantages, I'm not trying to discourage the use of worksheets. However, institute procedures and practices which ensure that forms and worksheets are properly used.

As in any data record, the signature and the date of entry are recorded at the time of the entry and represent and attest to the accuracy of the information. Any changes to the data or additional notes made after completion of the form or worksheet are made as previously described. Any unused lines on the form or worksheet should be crossed or 'Z'd' out. If the signature of a witness or reviewer is required, there should be a line allocated for this purpose.

Forms and worksheets can be a useful and practical way to record and preserve raw data – if you pay attention to the rules of data recording.

Automated data collection systems

This is the hottest and most difficult topic of this book. Application of data collection rules to computer systems has been the topic of seminars, books, journal articles, government policy committees, and regulatory interpretation. As an example of the policy difficulties, the FDA has spent the last several years trying to reach consensus on a policy for electronic signatures (US FDA, 1994).

Two major issues surround automated data collection systems: validation of the system and verification of the system's proper operation.

Validation asks whether the system is properly designed and tested so that it performs as it should to measure and record data accurately, completely, and consistently. In other words, are all the bugs worked out so that the system does not lose, change, or misrepresent the data you wish to obtain? I recall, from many years ago, a software program for recording animal weights. If a particular animal had died during the study and was not weighed at a weigh session, a '0' was entered for the weight. It was discovered that the software would automatically reject the 0 and record in its place the next animal's weight. This was totally unacceptable. The system was inadequately designed to handle commonly occurring data collection exceptions.

The second issue is the verification of the system's operation. Have you tested and proven that the data produced and recorded by the system are accurate, complete, and consistent, meeting all the date quality standards discussed under handwritten data?

Validation and verification are processes that involve hardware and software development, and acceptance testing, laboratory installation procedures and testing, computer security, and special record-keeping procedures, to name a few. There are numerous publications on this topic. If you are working in a research area subject to FDA or its equivalents, I suggest starting with the following: the *FDA Computerized Data Systems for Nonclinical Safety Assessment – Current Concepts and Quality Assurance*, known as the Red Apple Book, and the *FDA Technical Reference on Software Development Activities*.

The following sections will discuss the defining of raw data for automated data collection systems, what should be recorded in the raw data, electronic signatures, and report formats and spreadsheets.

Computer-generated raw data

It was my privilege to work with the author and a team of experts during the later stages of finalization of the GALPs (Good Automated Laboratory Practices). One of the most difficult tasks was deciding how to define raw data for laboratory information management systems (LIMS). Hours and days were spent on this issue alone. Here is the definition we ultimately used:

> *LIMS Raw Data are original observations recorded by the LIMS that are needed to verify, calculate, or derive data that are or may be reported. LIMS raw data storage media are the media to which LIMS Raw Data are first recorded.*

From these discussions, I have developed a broader-based alternative definition of computer-generated raw data. For automated data collection systems, 'raw data' mean the first record on the system of original observations that are human readable and that are needed to verify, calculate, or derive data that are or may be reported. The GALP definition was designed to fit the scope of the GALPs.

The real issue is how to apply the definition. Hand-recorded raw data are easy to define. What you see is what you write. Automated systems are much more complex. Analytical instruments may perform several functions – a transmitted light beam is measured, is converted into an electronic signal, this signal is transmitted to a computer, the software on the computer converts the signal to a machine-readable representation, this representation is translated into a value, this value is recorded into a report format that performs calculations and a summary of the input data, and the report is sent to an electronic file or to a printer.

The question is when do we have raw data? It is when an understandable value is first recorded. If the human-readable value is saved to a file prior to formatting, this is raw data. If the first recording of the data is in the report format, this is raw data. Some labs have declared the signal from the instrument to the computer to be raw data, but it is then very difficult to use the signal as a means for verification of the report of the data. This example represents only one situation of the possible variations in instrumentation. Each automated data collection system must be assessed to determine when the output is 'raw data'.

Why is the definition of raw data for computer applications so important? One obvious reason is to meet regulatory requirements. Behind these requirements are the same data quality characteristics that apply to hand-recorded data: accuracy, completeness, consistency, and reconstructability. As mentioned earlier, transcription of data can cause errors. Each time data are translated or reformatted by a software application, there is a potential for the data to be corrupted or lost. When the data are recorded and human readable *before* these operations, these 'raw data' can then be used to verify any subsequent iterations.

Here is the type of information that should be included in the automated raw data record:

- The instrument used to collect the data
- The person operating the instrument
- The date (and time) of the operation
- All conditions or settings for the instrument
- The person entering the data (if different from the operator)
- The date and time entered or reported
- The study title or code
- Cross-reference to a notebook or worksheet
- The measurements with associated sample identification
- All system-calculated results

If the system does not allow the input of any of the above information, it may be recorded by hand on the printout or on cross-referenced notebook pages or worksheets.

Automated raw data may be scored in soft copy (e.g. magnetic media) or in hard copy (e.g. paper printout, microfiche, microfilm). However, soft copy storage of raw data presents a unique set of problems that are often avoided by printing it in hard copy. Many labs choose to print out raw data, because it assures the data are available and unchanged. More about storage on magnetic media is discussed in Chapter 3.

Many software applications for instruments record the data in a worksheet format. The same rules as those for hand-generated worksheets should apply for automated formats. However, some raw data may not yet be formatted when they are first recorded. In this case, a key to the format of the raw data must accompany the data.

Why do we not designate the final formatted report as raw data in all cases? Remember, in the definition of raw data, the phrase, 'first recorded occurrence of the original observation'. This is important because the data should have undergone as little manipulation and transfer as possible over different software applications. This prevents corruption and loss and allows the raw data to be used to verify additional operations performed on it. Also, why not designate the signal read by the instrument or transmitted by the instrument as the raw data? Simply because it cannot be understood by humans and therefore is not useful to verify the results and conclusions. Testing should be performed on this signal, however, to validate the operation of the instrument and its communication functions.

Electronic signatures

Electronic signatures are the recorded identity of the individual entering data and are input through on-log procedures – presumed to be secure. One of the issues regarding electronic signatures is the validity of a computer-entered signature because it is not traceable by handwriting analysis to the signer, and presumably anyone could type in a name. One of the charges against Craven Labs was that the lab changed the clock on the computer to make it appear that samples were analyzed on an earlier date. Currently the FDA is accepting electronically recorded names or initials as signatures although the policy has not been made official at the time of writing.

Until a policy statement is made, two criteria may be used to justify the use of electronic signatures. All individuals who operate the instruments or associated software must be aware of the meaning and importance of the entry of their name (or unique personal code) and the computerized date stamp. That is what constitutes a legal signature. Second, the electronic signature is best justified when access to the system is strictly controlled. Controlled access usually involves some sort of password or user identification system that must be activated before an authorized person may perform an operation. Some automated systems have levels of access that may control different operations by allowing only certain individuals to perform certain tasks. Access levels may include read only, data entry, data change authorization, and system level entry or change. When these controls are in place, the system may automatically record the persons name into the file based on the password entered. Some systems use voice recognition or fingerprint recognition. This discussion only begins to touch on the complexities of computer security-related issues.

Spreadsheets

Spreadsheet use to the modern lab is what invention of the printing press was to publication. Although spreadsheets make recording, processing, and reporting data easy and quick, some special considerations are important to the use of these powerful programs. Whether data are keyed into spreadsheets or electronically transferred to them from existing data files, the entry of the data must be checked to assure the data record is complete and correct. Commonly, mistakes occur in calculations and formulas, in designating data fields, and in performing inappropriate operations on the data. Because of the versatility of spreadsheets, take special care in validating the spreadsheet. When you perform calculations, check the spreadsheet formulas and be sure that the arithmetic formula is defined on the spreadsheet. The way the program rounds numbers and reports significant digits is important to the calculation of results and the reporting of the data. When you try to recalculate or evaluate the processes performed by the spreadsheet program, be sure to define all functions.

REPORTING THE DATA

This final section suggests ways to generate data tables and figures for the final report or manuscript. Here are some guidelines:

- The title of the table or figure should be descriptive of the data.
- Column and row headings should be understandable, avoiding undefined abbreviations.
- Units of measure should be included in the column headings or axes of charts.
- For individual data, all missing values must be footnoted and explained.
- All calculations used to derive the data should be defined and, when the calculation is complex or nonstandard, given in a footnote.
- Statistical summaries or analyses should be clearly defined including the type of process performed. Statistically significant values may be identified with a unique symbol that is footnoted.
- All but the most common abbreviations should be defined.
- Continuing pages should contain at least a descriptive portion of the title and indicate 'continued'.
- The data should be easy to read and be uncluttered.

THE SELECTION AND USE OF CROs

- Charts should contain a legend of any symbols or colors used, and the labels of the axes should be descriptive and easily understood.
- The text of the report should include references to the tables or figures when the data is presented.
- The text of the report should exactly match the data in the tables or figures. Any generalization, summarization, or significant rounding should be designated as such in the text.

Distinguishing essential from negotiable study elements

An important step is to determine which parts of the study must be included. It is desirable to maximize the amount of information to be obtained, while also considering time, number of animals, and use of other resources. It may not be realistic to try to accomplish all the objectives which can be stated during the early stages of study design. This distinction of essential and negotiable study elements is a critical step which will enable the study sponsor to select a suitable laboratory as well as to negotiate the specific components of the study.

Designating the study monitor

Another early aspect to consider in external placement concerns personnel, specifically, the study's director. In the past, it was not uncommon that the employee or consultant who functions as a study monitor on behalf of the sponsor would be called the 'study director'. This is now a difficult concept to grasp, since the responsibilities of the study director imply being intimately involved with and overseeing the day-to-day activities of the study and can therefore be discharged only by an employee of the laboratory contracted to perform the study. Regardless of what the on-site study director is called, the sponsor needs to provide sufficient authority to allow important decisions to be made without prolonged discussions on the telephone, or worse yet, emergency site visits by the sponsor and for clean lines of authority for any potential changes.

For complex or long-term studies, the laboratory should provide an alternate study director to ensure both continuing internal oversight as well as a contact for the sponsor if the primary study director is unavailable.

Having defined the work to be done, ranked the elements of the study as essential or negotiable, and selected a study monitor from within the sponsor's organization, a laboratory must be found which can do the necessary work.

REFERENCES

DeWoskin, R.S. (1995). *Quality Assurance SOPs for GLP Compliance*, Interpharm Press, Buffalo Grove, IL.

Drug Information Association (2002). *2002 Contract Service Organization Directory*. DIA, Fort Washington, PA.

EPA (1989a). FIFRA Good Laboratory Practice Standards, Final Rule, *Fed. Reg.* **54**, 34052–34074.

EPA (1989b). FIFRA Good Laboratory Practice Standards, Final Rule, *Fed. Reg.* **52**, 48933–48946.

FDA (1984). *Compliance Program Guidance Manual*, Chapter 48, Human drugs and biologics: Bio research monitoring. FDA, Washington, DC.

FDA (1987). Good Laboratory Practice Regulations, Final Rule, *Fed. Reg.* **52**, 33768–33782.

FDA (1994). Electronic Signatures; Electronic Records; Proposed Rule, *Fed. Reg.* **59**, 13200.

FDA (1997a). Electronic Signatures; Electronic Records; Final Rule, 21 *CFR* Part 11.

FDA (1997b). Electronic Submissions, Establishment of Public Docket; 21 *CFR* Part 11.

FDA (2002a). *Code of Federal Regulations*, Title 21, Part 58 (Food, Drug and Cosmetic Act).

FDA (2002b). To obtain inspection reports from FDA, one can call their FOI office at (301) 443–6310. The mail address for such is: Department of Health and Human Services, 200 Independence Ave., SW, Washington, DC 20201.

FDA (2002c). Food and Drug Administration's 2002 *Code of Federal Regulations* are available on-line at http://www.gmppublications.com.

Freudenthal, R.I. (1997). *Directory of Toxicology Laboratories Offering Contract Service*. Aribel Books, West Palm Beach, FL.

Gad, S.C. (2001). *Regulatory Toxicology*, 2nd edn., Taylor & Francis, Philadelphia, PA.

JACKSON, E.M. (1985). *International Directory of Contract Laboratories.* Marcel Dekker, Inc, New York.

TEXAS RESEARCH INSTITUTE (1986). *Directory of Toxicology Testing Institutions.* Texas Research Institute, Houston.

ADDITIONAL READING

Drug Information Association. *Computerized Data Systems for Non-Clinical Safety Assessments: Current Concepts and Quality Assurance.* Maple Glen, PA, September 1988.

FDA, Good Clinical Practices: *CFR*, Title 21, Part 50, 56, 312, April 1, 1993.

FDA (1976). Good Laboratory Practice Regulations original proposal, *Fed. Reg.* **41**, 51206–51230. This details the reasons for the proposed GLPs and includes a catalog of deficiencies found in laboratories which performed studies in support of FDA regulated products.

FDA, Current Good Manufacturing Practices for Finished Pharmaceuticals, *CFR*, Title 21, Part 211.

FDA, Current Good Manufacturing Practices for Medical Devices, General, *CFR*, Title 21, Part 820.

FDA, Guide for Detecting Fraud in Bioresearch Monitoring Inspections, Office of Regulatory Affairs, US FDA, April 1993.

GAD, S.C. and TAULBEE, S.M. (1996). *Handbook of Data Recording, Maintenance, and Management for the Biomedical Sciences.* CRC Press, Boca Raton, FL.

GRALLA, E.J. (ed.) (1981). *Scientific Considerations in Monitoring and Evaluating Toxicological Research.* Hemisphere Publishing Corporation, Washington, DC.

Guide for the Care and Use of Laboratory Animals, DHEW Publ. No. (NIH) 78–23, revised 1985.

Guide to the Care and Use of Laboratory Animals, National Institutes of Health, Bethesda, MD, 1985–1986.

HOOVER, B.K., BALDWIN, J.K., UELNER, A.F., WHITMIRE, C.E., DAVIES, C.L., and BRISTOL, D.W. (eds) (1986). *Managing Conduct and Data Quality of Toxicology Studies.* Princeton Scientific Publishing Co., Inc, Princeton.

Institutional Animal Care and Use Committee Guidebook, NIH Pub. No. 92–3415. U.S. Department of Health and Human Services, pp. E33–37.

JACKSON, E.M. (1984). How to choose a contract laboratory: Utilizing a laboratory clearance procedure. *J. Toxicol. Cut. Ocular Toxicol.* **3**, 83–92.

JAMES, J.W. (1982). *Good Laboratory Practice*, ChemTech, 1962–1965, March 1982.

PAGET, G.E. (1977). *Quality Control in Toxicology*. University Park Press, Baltimore, MD.

PAGET, G.E. (1979). *Good Laboratory Practice*. University Park Press, Baltimore, MD.

PAGET, G.E. and THOMPSON, R. (eds) (1979a). *Standard Operating Procedures in Toxicology*. University Park Press, Baltimore, MD.

PAGET, G.E. and THOMPSON, R. (eds) (1979b). *Standard Operating Procedures in Pathology*. University Park Press, Baltimore, MD.

TAULBEE, S.M. and DEWOSKIN, R.S. (1993). *Taulbee's Pocket Companion: U.S. FDA and DPA GLPs in Parallel*. Interpharm Press, Buffalo Grove, IL.

The Pharmaceutical Development Process

The process by which a new therapeutic entity is discovered and developed to the point that it is available to patients in the marketplace is complex, expensive and long. I will not pretend to present or analyze this process in any detail here, but rather to give a basic understanding of the process and of the components which may be outsourced to a contract organization. There are no current or comprehensive volumes describing this process, though there are some volumes on the area (Sneader, 1986; Guarino, 1987; Smith, 1992; Spilker, 1994; Mathieu, 2000).

As explained at the beginning of this volume, the pharmaceutical development process is a long (13–16 years from drug inception to market approval) and costly ($250 million to $800 million, depending on how one allocates costs) process, even when successful. It is shaped by medical needs, regulatory requirements, economics, our understanding of sciences and diseases, and limitations of technology. All of these interact to shape a process which serves to reduce risks iteratively (to both economic and human safety), with the probability of failure being reduced in a stepwise fashion (Matoren, 1984; Zbinden, 1992). Figure 2.1 briefly summarizes this process, while Figure 2.2 presents a more detailed summary of the process and activities up to the filing of an IND (Investigative New Drug Application) and Figure 2.3 an alternative presentation. I will use the six categories of activities in that figure (Safety, Pharmaceutical Development, Pharmacology, Analytical, Clinical and Regulatory) as a framework to discuss activities throughout the development process. The major pharmaceutical companies [generally seen as the members of Pharmaceutical Research and Manufacturers of America, PhRMA (Table 2.1)] have their research and development expenses well documented (Table 2.2 and 2.3). These figures are impressive, as are the sales of their products (Table 2.4). It should be kept in mind, however, that there are more than 2500 smaller pharmaceutical development companies (both 'small molecule' and biotech) in the United States which have an even higher proportion of their budgets invested annually in research and development.

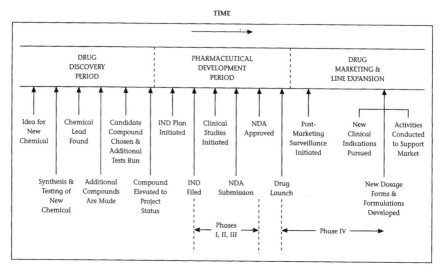

Figure 2.1: Generalized flow of pharmaceutical development.

For our purposes (that is, from the development to market perspective), the purpose of all nonclinical (animal and *in vitro*) development is to reduce the risks and probability of adverse events while optimizing the potential for therapeutic efficiency in humans. But between initial nonclinical testing (and concurrent with additional animal testing) and a drug's reaching the marketplace, the potential for having adverse effects in the general patient population it is intended for is further guarded against by a scheme of increasingly more powerful human (or 'clinical') trials (Piantadosi, 1997; Nylen, 2000). How a drug is moved through this process is the subject of this chapter.

SAFETY

The safety component of the development of a new drug has both a nonclinical (that is, not in human beings) and a clinical component. Until an IND is opened, all safety evaluation is nonclinical (also properly called, to this point, preclinical). After an IND is opened, both clinical and nonclinical components of safety evaluation are required. The timing of the nonclinical components, particularly after an IND is opened, is open to a fair degree of judgment. Details of the components of this process are beyond the scope of this volume (see Gad, 2002 for such details).

Time (Months)	Safety	Pharmaceutical Development	Pharmacology	Analytical	Clinical	Regulatory
Needed to Start ↑		xg — non-GMP Compound	In Vivo dfficacy (1st Species)			Define Claim
0	Acute Tox -Mouse(iv&po) -Rat -Dog			Develop GLP Analytical		
1	CYP Screen Metabolic Profile Genotox -Ames -Micronucleus -CHO Chromosome Abber.		CACO-2 Screen			
2		ykg GMP		Develop GLP Bioanalytical –2 Species + Humans		
3						Pre-IND Meeting
4	Protein Binding		In Vivo Efficacy (2nd Species)	Drug Stability -Reference Standards -Set Specs		
5	28-day Rodent with Pharma-cokinetics / 28-day non-rodent with Pharma-cokinetics / Safety Pharma-cology	Make CTM			Phase I Protocol Investigators Brochure Informed Consent CRF Development	
6	Rat Seg II Pilot					
7						
8						
9						
10						Write IND
11						File IND
12						

Figure 2.2: Components of development to the filing and opening of an IND.

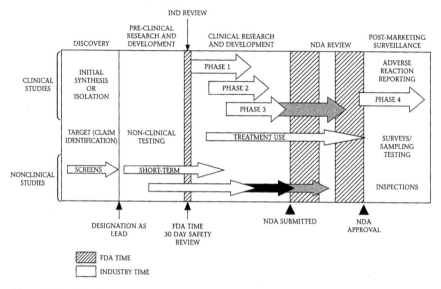

Figure 2.3: The pharmaceutical development process, viewed as four stages (discovery, preclinical development, clinical development, and NDA review) as well as the important post-market surveillance phase.

All the safety evaluation components have in common that they are heavily regulated and subject to either GLPs (Good Laboratory Practices) or GCPs (Good Clinical Practices). The nonclinical components include genotoxicity (a minimum of three studies, usually an ames, assay and CHO chromosome aberration or unscheduled DNA synthesis *in vitro* and a mouse micronucleus *in vivo*), safety pharmacology (with evaluations of cardio-vascular, central nervous system and respiratory pharmacologic activities being required pre-IND and others before large clinical trials in patients are initiated), immunotoxicology (just now coming into being specifically required), systemic toxicity (single and multiple dose in two or more species with a pharmacokinetic component to the multidose pre-IND, then longer multiple dose studies in concert with clinical development), developmental and reproductive toxicity, carcinogenicity evaluations (if the drug is intended to be for chronic use) and any special studies that may be specific to the class of drugs or its use. Also generally required are determinations of protein binding, the pharmacokinetics of the drug in animals and man, metabolic activation and inhibition, and nature of significant metabolites in man (Ozdemir *et al.*, 2001).

TABLE 2.1
PhRMA member companies

Abbott Laboratories *Abbott Park, IL*	Fujisawa Healthcare, Inc. *Deerfield, IL*	Merck & Co., Inc. *Whitehouse Station, NJ*
Allergan, Inc. *Irvine, CA*	Genzyme Corporation *Cambridge, MA*	Novartis Pharmaceuticals Corporation *E. Hanover, NJ*

American Home Products
Corporation
Madison, NJ
  Wyeth-Ayerst
  Pharmaceuticals
  Wyeth-Ayerst Research
	Gilead Sciences, Inc.
	Foster City, CA
	
	GlaxoSmithKline
	Research Triangle Park, NC
		Organon Inc.
		West Orange, NJ
		
		Otsuka America
		Pharmaceutical, Inc.
		Rockville, MD

Amersham Health *Princeton, NJ*	Hoffmann-La Roche Inc. *Nutley, NJ*	Pfizer Inc. *New York, NY*
Amgen Inc. *Thousand Oaks, CA*	Johnson & Johnson *New Brunswick, NJ* Advanced Sterilization	Pharmacia Corporation

AstraZeneca LP
Wilmington, DE
	Products
	  ALZA Corporation
	  Centocor, Inc.
		Peapack, NJ
		
		The Procter & Gamble

Aventis Pharma AG
Bridgewater, NJ
  Aventis Pasteur
  Aventis Pharmaceuticals,
  Inc.
	Cordis Corporation
	  DePuy Inc.
	  Ethicon Endo-Surgery, Inc.
	  Ethicon, Inc.
	  • Ethicon Products
	  • Gynecare
	  • Johnson & Johnson
		Company
		Procter & Gamble
		Pharmaceuticals, Inc.
		Mason, OH
		
		Purdue Pharma L.P.

Bayer Corporation
Pharmaceutical Division
West Haven, CT
	Wound
	  Management
	  Janssen Pharmaceutica
		Stamford, CT
		
		Sanofi-Synthelabo Inc.

Berlex Laboratories, Inc.
Montville, NJ (effective 4/02)
	Inc.
	  Janssen Research
	  Foundation and The
		New York, NY
		
		Schering-Plough

Biogen, Inc.
Cambridge, MA
	R.W. Johnson
	  Pharmaceutical Research
	  Institute
		Corporation
		Kenilworth, NJ

Bio-Technology General Corp.
Iselin, NJ
	Johnson & Johnson Health
	  Care Systems, Inc.
	  Mitek
		SCHWARZ PHARMA,
		INC.
		Mequon, WI

Boehringer Ingelheim
Pharmaceuticals, Inc.
Ridgefield, CT
	Ortho Biotech Products,
	  L.P.
	  Ortho-Clinical Diagnostics
		Serono, Inc.
		Norwell, MA

Bristol-Myers Squibb
Company
New York, NY
	Ortho Dermatological
	  Ortho-McNeil
	  Pharmaceutical, Inc.
	  Therakos, Inc.
	  Vistakon
		Solvay Pharmaceuticals,
		Inc.
		Marietta, GA
		  Unimed
		  Pharmaceuticals, Inc.

Elan Pharmaceuticals, Inc. *South San Francisco, CA*	Eli Lilly and Company *Indianapolis, IN*	3M Pharmaceuticals *St. Paul, MN*

TABLE 2.2

Growth in domestic R&D and R&D abroad, ethical pharmaceuticals, PhRMA member companies, 1970–2001

Year	Domestic R&D ($)	Annual Percentage Change	R&D Abroad ($)	Annual Percentage Change	Total R&D ($)	Annual Percentage Change
*2001	23 887.8	11.8	6454.9	38.3	30 342.7	16.6
2000	21 363.7	15.7	4667.1	10.6	26 030.8	14.7
1999	18 471.1	7.4	4219.6	9.9	22 690.7	8.2
1998	17 127.9	11.0	3839.0	9.9	20 966.9	10.8
1997	15 466.0	13.9	3492.1	6.5	18 958.1	12.4
1996	13 627.1	14.8	3278.5	-1.6	16 905.6	11.2
1995	11 874.0	7.0	3333.5	**	15 207.4	**
1994	11 101.6	6.0	2347.8	3.8	13 449.4	5.6
1993	10 477.1	12.5	2262.9	5.0	12 740.0	11.1
1992	9312.1	17.4	2155.8	21.3	11 467.9	18.2
1991	7928.6	16.5	1776.8	9.9	9705.4	15.3
1990	6802.9	13.0	1617.4	23.6	8420.3	14.9
1989	6021.4	15.0	1308.6	0.4	7330.0	12.1
1988	5233.9	16.2	1303.6	30.6	6537.5	18.8
1987	4504.1	16.2	998.1	15.4	5502.2	16.1
1986	3875.0	14.7	865.1	23.8	4740.1	16.2
1985	3378.7	13.3	698.9	17.2	4077.6	13.9
1984	2982.4	11.6	596.4	9.2	3578.8	11.2
1983	2671.3	17.7	546.3	8.2	3217.6	16.0
1982	2268.7	21.3	505.0	7.7	2773.7	18.6
1981	1870.4	20.7	469.1	9.7	2339.5	18.4
1980	1549.2	16.7	427.5	42.8	1976.7	21.5
1979	1327.4	13.8	299.4	25.9	1626.8	15.9
1978	1166.1	9.7	237.9	11.6	1404.0	10.0
1977	1063.0	8.1	213.1	18.2	1276.1	9.7
1976	983.4	8.8	180.3	14.1	1163.7	9.6
1975	903.5	13.9	158.0	7.0	1061.5	12.8
1974	793.1	12.0	147.7	26.3	940.8	14.0
1973	708.1	8.1	116.9	64.0	825.0	13.6
1972	654.8	4.5	71.3	24.9	726.1	6.2
1971	626.7	10.7	57.1	9.2	683.8	10.6
1970	566.2	–	52.3	–	618.5	–
Average		12.9		16.8		13.5

* Estimated. ** R&D Abroad affected by merger and acquisition activity.
Notes: 1. R&D expenditures for ethical pharmaceuticals only. 2. Domestic R&D includes expenditures within the United States by PhRMA member companies.
3. R&D Abroad includes expenditures outside the United States by US-owned PhRMA member companies and R&D conducted abroad by US divisions of foreign-owned PhRMA member companies. 4. Increases in R&D expenditures are likely due to a more rigorous data collection methodology.
Source: Pharmaceutical Research and Manufacturers of America, PhRMA Annual Membership Survey, 2002.

TABLE 2.3

Domestic R&D by function, ethical pharmaceuticals, PhRMA member companies, 1998–2000 (dollar figures in millions)

Function	1998		1999		2000	
	Dollars	Share (%)	Dollars	Share (%)	Dollars	Share (%)
Synthesis and Extraction	2066.7	12.07	1763.1	10.0	987.7	9.3
Biological Screening and Pharmacological Testing	2600.5	15.1	2508.1	14.2	2582.9	12.1
Toxicology and Safety Testing	895.5	5.2	802.1	4.5	872.1	4.1
Pharmaceutical Dosage Formulation and Stability Testing	1550.0	9.0	1290.6	7.3	1081.3	5.1
Clinical Evaluation: Phase I, II, and III	4873.9	28.3	5139.5	29.1	5464.6	25.6
Clinical Evaluation: Phase IV	998.9	5.8	2060.5	11.7	1882.3	8.8
Process Development for Manufacturing and Quality Control	1705.0	9.9	1463.4	8.3	1499.9	7.0
Regulatory: IND and NDA	757.7	4.4	730.3	4.1	644.2	3.0
Bioavailability	413.4	2.4	321.6	1.8	327.8	1.5
Other R&D	1265.9	7.9	1594.3	9.0	2693.7	12.6
Uncategorized Ethical Pharmaceutical R&D*	0.4	0.0	797.6	4.3	2327.2	10.9
Total	17 127.9	100	18 471.1	100	21 363.7	100

* Represents companies that provided total R&D expenditure figures, but not individual details.
Notes: 1. Company-financed R&D expenditures for ethical pharmaceuticals only. 2. Domestic R&D includes expenditures within the Unites States by PhRMA member companies.
Source: *Pharmaceutical Research and Manufacturers of America, PhRMA Annual Membership Survey, 2002.*

TABLE 2.4

Top pharmaceutical companies

Company	Annual revenue (2001) ($)	R&D expenditures (2001) ($)
Pfizer	25.5 billion	4.8 billion
GlaxoSmithKline	24.7 billion	3.8 billion
Merck	20.5 billion	2.5 billion
AstraZenca	16.5 billion	2.7 billion
Bristol-Myers Squibb	16.3 billion	2.3 billion
Aventis	15.7 billion	2.6 billion
Johnson & Johnson	14.9 billion	3.6 billion
Novartis	13.5 billion	2.5 billion
Pharmacia	12.0 billion	2.3 billion
Wyeth	11.7 billion	1.9 billion
Eli Lilly & Co.	10.9 billion	2.2 billion
Abbot Laboratories	9.0 billion	1.3 billion
F. Hoffman-La Roche	8.5 billion	2.3 billion
Schering-Plough	8.4 billion	1.3 billion
Takeda Chemical Industries	5.8 billion	756 million
Sanofi-Synthelabo	5.6 billion	913 million
Bayer AG	5.1 billion	2.3 billion
Boehringer-Ingelheim	4.7 billion	903 million
Sankyo Co.	3.2 billion	615 million
*Amgen	3.5 billion	526 million
Shionogi & Co.	3.0 billion	230 million
*Genentech	1.7 billion	207 million
*Serono	1.2 billion	309 million
*Immunex	960 million	205 million
*Biogen	972 million	314 million
*Genzyme General	831 million	138 million
*Chiron	703 million	344 million
*MedImmune	580 million	83 million
*Celltech Group	351 million	132 million
Gilead Sciences	191 million	186 million

* Indicates biopharmaceutical companies.

PHARMACEUTICAL DEVELOPMENT

The chemical development process also stretches through most of the length of the pharmaceutical development process. The needs to be met include:

1 Manufacture of increasing quantities of active pharmaceutical ingredient of suitable purity and stability. Early lots are in gram (or tens of grams) quantities for small molecules. Such are produced under GLPs but not GMPs. Frequently the first upscale produces lots of hundreds of grams.

Finally, lots of a kilo or greater size are produced. Somewhere in here the most stabile (and possibly soluble) form (frequently a salt) is produced under GMPs. Later efforts still may seek to identify the most economical production process.

2   Human dosage form(s) must be developed and produced. When used in clinical trials, these are labeled CTM (clinical test material). If for an oral drug, a simple formulation (such as a stability, simple capsule vial) may be used for phase I studies, but more elegant formulations are produced for later studies. If the route is parenteral, simple sterile, stability, and isotonic solutions are employed.

3   Formulations must be developed, first for preclincial studies and then for clinical studies. Lots of considerations come into such formulations including bioavailability, stability, use of allowed excipients, and patient acceptability.

Swarbrick and Boylan (2002) provide an excellent overview of the range of skills and technology involved here.

PHARMACOLOGY

Pharmacology studies (other than safety pharmacology) initially serve to identify candidate compounds for development. Such studies (particularly in appropriate 'gold standard' models of the specific disease to be treated – or predictive of such) are essential both in making decisions to go forward with development of a compound and in helping estimate or model the dose to be used in the clinic. Dose selection or 'target identification' for clinical trials is best performed based on achieving a concentration of therapeutic entity at the target site (receptors or organs *in vivo*), but should at least have achieved plasma levels at efficient doses at the target for clinical studies.

Additionally, it is important to evaluate the specificity of action at the target sites. This means that activity and or binding at other receptor sites must be quantitated, as such may limit the potential utility of a drug.

ANALYTICAL

It is clearly essential to be able to both identify and quantitate the actual drug entity itself in a range of venues. These include the lots of drug produced (where purity and the identity of any accompanying impurities also is important), stability study samples, dosage preparations for preclinical studies, and fluid and tissue samples from *in vivo* studies.

The last of these usually means being able to quantitate accurately and sensitively the levels of the drug entity in plasma and urine, and possibly in target tissues. Such methods must be developed and validated not only for humans but also for the principal species used in nonclinical studies (usually rats and either dogs or primates, plus in rabbits to verify exposure in developmental toxicology studies).

It also becomes important at some point to be able to identify and quantitate the levels of significant metabolites, particularly if they are pharmacologically active.

CLINICAL

Generally the single most expensive (and time consuming) portion of pharmaceutical development is the clinical evaluation (Spilker, 1994). Initially these studies (phase I) are intended primarily to evaluate the safety (tolerance) and pharmacokinetics of a drug, and unless the drug is intended to treat life-threatening conditions such studies are performed in healthy volunteers and not patients. While it should generally be possible to perform such work with three (single dose escalating, multidose tolerance and a single dose escalating) or four studies (validation of achieved dose by an optimized formulation/dosage form), many more may be performed.

Subsequently, a series of phase II studies are generally performed in patients, initially to give confidence in efficacy. It should be noted that approval generally requires two successful 'pivotal' studies. These are usually phase III studies, but may be phase II. The requirements are: adequate numbers of patients to achieve statistical proof of efficacy in an accepted *a priori* endpoint, and adequate numbers and exposure of a representative patient population to identify significant safety concerns when the drug is on the market; while protecting trial subject safety to the fullest extent possible (Willman, 2000; Wechsler, 2001).

This clinical testing phase is almost always both the longest and most expensive segment of the drug development portion. From the earliest point, sponsors/investigators are looking for a reliable hint that the drug works (see Biomarkers Definitions Working Group, 2001) while also worrying about previously undetected safety concerns such as hepatic damage (Kaplowilz, 2001).

REGULATORY

In parallel with all of the technical activities which are included in the pharmaceutical development process, there is an accompanying string of activities which must be conducted to fulfill the regulatory requirements for successfully completing the process. These usually start with bringing about a successful pre-IND meeting with the FDA. Subsequent to this, the following are generally necessary:

1 An INDA must be assembled, paginated and submitted. Any resulting questions raised by the FDA must be answered effectively and in a very timely manner.
2 The 'opening' of the IND must be verified.
3 Necessary IND amendments (documenting changes in formulation; significant findings as to safety; changes in clinical study protocols, facilities or personnel or new protocols) must be submitted in a timely manner.
4 An end of phase II meeting with the FDA should be effectively executed.
5 Assembly and submission of an NDA, with effective and timely response to any subsequent FDA queries.
6 An effective quality monitoring and auditing program of vendors performing GLP, GMP and/or GCP regulated tasks.

Except for those cases where there is substantial potential to save or extend lives (such as anticancer and anti-AIDS drugs) or where the intended target diseases are chronic and severe (Parkinson's or MS) or the routes of administration are invasive (intrathecal), the initial evaluations in humans are performed in 'normal' healthy volunteers with the primary objective being limited to defining the limits of tolerance (safety) of the potential drug and its pharmacokinetic characteristics. These trials may also seek to detect limited (usually surrogate, that is, indirect) indicators of efficacy, but are severely limited in doing so (Biomarker Definitions Working Group, 2001). Later trials look at the drug's actions on carefully defined groups of patients.

With the number of drugs withdrawn from the marketplace since 1990 (or, perhaps, the degree of media coverage of such withdrawals), public concern with the workings of the drug safety evaluation aspects of the development process has risen sharply (Granter, 1999; Wechsler, 2001). It is currently estimated that in the United States, adverse drug reactions (ADRs) rank between the fourth and sixth leading cause of death (Eikelboom *et al.*, 2001). While improvements in the nonclinical aspects of drug safety assessments are possible and even likely, clearly the clinical aspects are likely to be where most improvement in trials and a better understanding of individual or subpopulation differences in human responses to drugs are to be found.

While there is much press about the concern that the 'increased pace of drug approval' has caused the release onto the market of less safe drugs (Willman, 2000), the causes are more mundane and of much longer standing. The most common 'unexpected' (from nonclinical trial results) safety findings in initial trials involve the skin (dermatitis of one form or another) and liver (Kaplowilz, 2001). An important reason for the high incidence of serious and fatal ADRs is that the existing drug development paradigms do not generate adequate information on the mechanistic sources of marked variability in pharmaco-kinetics and pharmacodynamics of new therapeutic candidates, precluding treatments from being tailored for individual patients (Ozdemir *et al.*, 2001).

Pharmacogenetics is the study of the hereditary basis of person-to-person variations in drug response. The focus of pharmacogenetic investigations has traditionally been unusual and extreme drug responses resulting from a single gene effect. The Human Genome Project and recent advancements in molecular genetics now present an unprecedented opportunity to study all genes in the human genome, including genes for drug metabolism, drug targets, and post-receptor second messenger mechanisms, in relation to variability in drug safety and efficacy. In addition to sequence variations in the genome, high throughput and genome-wide transcript profiling for differentially regulated mRNA species before and during drug treatment will serve as important tools to uncover novel mechanisms of drug action. Pharmacogenetic-guided drug discovery and development represent a departure for the conventional approach which markets drugs for broad patient populations, rather than smaller groups of patients in whom drugs may work more optimally. To date, these tools have not brought a product to market. But their use is in demand, as are the older receptor-binding screening services intended to determine the specificity of action of a potential drug.

PUTTING IT ALL TOGETHER

While not a separate or distinct segment of pharmaceutical development, the need for integrative project management services to ensure that all the pieces (whether of clinical trials or the entire development process) are brought together is both clearly essential and an area where extensive contract services are available. In the large pharmaceutical companies (Table 2.1 and 2.4), these skills are internal. For the vast majority of the smaller 2000+ pharmaceutical/ biotech companies this is not the case and the services must be contracted in part or whole from either a large ('meta') CRO, a smaller provider specializing in such, or a 'boutique' organization which serves only a few clients at a time.

REFERENCES

Biomarkers Definitions Working Group (2001). Biomarkers and surrogate endpoints: Preferred definitions and conceptual frameworks. *Clin. Pharmacol. Ther.* **69**, 89–95.

EIKELBOOM, J.W., MEHTA, S.R., POGUE, J., and YUSUF, S. (2001). Safety Outcomes in Meta-analyses of Phase II versus Phase III Randomized Trials. *JAMA* **285**, 444–450.

GAD, S.C. (2002). *Drug Safety Evaluation.* Wiley & Sons, New York.

GRANTER, J. (1999). Responding to industry critics: If the industry doesn't address concerns raised by the consumer press, who will? *Appl. Clini. Trials* 10, November, pp. 18–22.

GUARINO, R.A. (1987). *New Drug Approval Process.* Marcel Dekker, New York.

KAPLOWILZ, N. (2001). Drug induced liver disorders: Implications for drug development and regulation. *Drug Information Journal* **35**, 347–400.

MATHIEU, M. (2000). *New Drug Development: A regulatory Overview.* Parexel, Waltham, MA.

MATOREN, G.M. (1984). *The Clinical Research Process in the Pharmaceutical Industry.* Marcel Dekker, New York.

NYLEN, R.A. (2000). *The Ultimate Step-By-Step Guide to Conducting Pharmaceutical Clinical Trials in the USA.* RAN Institute, Tampa, FL.

OZDEMIR, V., SHEAR, N.H., and KALOW, W. (2001). What will be the role of pharmacokinetics in evaluating drug safety and minimizing adverse effects? *Drug Safety* **24**, 75–85.

PIANTADOSI, S. (1997). *Clinical Trials: A Methadoligic Perspective.* John Wiley & Sons, New York.

SMITH, C.G. (1992). *The Process of New Drug Discovery and Development.* CRC Press, Boca Raton, FL.

SNEADER, W. (1986). *Drug Development: From Laboratory to Clinic.* John Wiley & Sons, New York.

SPILKER, B. (1994). *Multinational Pharmaceutical Companies*. Raven Press, New York.

SWARBRICK, J. and BOYLAN, J.C. (2002). *Encyclopedia of Pharmaceutical Technology*, 2nd edn, Marcel Dekker, New York.

WECHSLER, J. (2001). Clinical trial safety and oversight top policy agenda. *Appl. Clin. Trials.*, January 2001, pp. 18–21.

WILLMAN, D. (2000). Quickened pace of drug approvals by FDA taking toll. *San Jose Mercury News*, p. 1a, Dec. 28.

ZBINDEN, G. (1992). *The Source of the River Po*. Haag & Herchen, Frankfurt am Main, Germany.

The Medical Device Development Process

The medical device industry in the United States and worldwide is immense in its economic impact (sales in 1998 were $138 billion worldwide, and $59 billion in the United States, $34 billion in the European Community, and $23 billion in Japan; in 1998, the US medical equipment trade surplus was $8.7 billion), scope (between 87 000 and 140 000 different devices are produced in the United States by approximately 8200 different manufacturers employing some 311 000 people; it is believed that more than 1000 of these manufacturers are development-stage companies without products yet on the market), and importance to the health of the world's citizens (Nugent, 1994; the Wilkerson Group, 1999) (Table 3.1). Large companies dominate sales, but (as in pharmaceuticals) not innovation. The assessment of the safety to patients using the multitude of items produced by this industry is dependent on schemes and methods that are largely peculiar to these kinds of products, are not as rigorous as those employed for foods, drugs, and pesticides, and are in a state of flux. Regulation of such devices is, in fact, relatively new. It is only with the Medical Device Amendments (to the Food, Drug and Cosmetic Act) of 1976 that devices have come to be explicitly regulated at all, and with the Safe Medical Devices Act of 1990, the Medical Device Amendments of 1992, and subsequent laws that the regulation of devices for biocompatibility became rigorous (see Table 3.2). According to section 201(h) of the Food, Drug and Cosmetic Act, a medical device is an instrument, apparatus, implement,

TABLE 3.1

The largest medical device markets (2001)

	US $ in billions
Diagnostics (*in vitro*)	20.5
Surgery (minimally invasive)	16.4
Orthopedic	14.7
Wound care	13.0
Cardiovascular	12.5

TABLE 3.2

FDA Classification of preamendment medical devices

Part No.	Title	Date of Publication
21 C.F.R. Part 862	Clinical chemistry and clinical toxicology	May 1, 1987
21 C.F.R. Part 864	Hematology and pathology devices	May 11, 1987
21 C.F.R. Part 866	Immunology and microbiology	November 9, 1982
21 C.F.R. Part 868	Anesthesiology devices	July 16, 1982
21 C.F.R. Part 870	Cardiovascular devices	February 5, 1980
21 C.F.R. Part 872	Dental devices	August 12, 1987
21 C.F.R. Part 874	Ear, nose and throat devices	November 6, 1986
21 C.F.R. Part 876	Gastroenterology-urology devices	November 23, 1983
21 C.F.R. Part 878	General and plastic surgery devices	June 24, 1988
21 C.F.R. Part 880	General hospital and personal use	October 21, 1980
21 C.F.R. Part 882	Neurological devices	November 4, 1979
21 C.F.R. Part 884	Obstetrical and gynecological devices	February 26, 1980
21 C.F.R Part 886	Ophthalmic devices	September 2, 1987
21 C.F.R. Part 888	Orthopedic devices	September 4, 1987
21 C.F.R. Part 890	Physical medicine devices	November 23, 1983
21 C.F.R. Part 892	Radiological devices	January 20, 1988

- FDA determines that the device is substantially equivalent to another device that was not in commercial distribution before such date but that has since been classified into Class I or II (through the 510(k) process); or
- FDA reclassifies the device into Class I or II.

machine, contrivance, implant, *in vitro* reagent, or other similar or related article, including a component, part, or accessory that is

- Recognized in the official National Formulary, or the United States Pharmacopoeia (USP, 2000), or any supplement to them.
- Intended for use in the diagnosis of disease, in man or other animals.
- Intended to affect the structure or any function of the body of man or other animals, and that does not achieve any of its primary intended purposes through chemical action within or on the body of man or other animals, and that is not dependent upon being metabolized for the achievement of any of its principal intended purposes (CDRH, 1992).

The procedures for reclassifying a 'postamendment' Class III device are codified in 21 C.F.R. section 860.134(b)(1)–(7).

The device classification process continues to this day. As the FDA becomes aware of new devices that require formal classification or pre-1976 devices that were somehow overlooked in the original classification procedures, the agency initiates new classification proceedings, again requesting the recommendation of one or more of the appropriate advisory panels.

TABLE 3.3

The 10 projected biggest growth device products in 2000

Rank	Product	Percentage revenue growth rate (years)	Specialty
1	Fibrin sealants	174.6 (95–02)	Wound care
2	Solid artificial organs	141.2 (95–02)	Transplant/implant
3	Left ventricular assist devices	96.0 (95–02)	Cardiovascular
4	Skin substitute products	63.1 (97–04)	Wound care
5	Refractive surgical devices	54.4 (98–05)	Ophthalmic
6	Gynecologic fallopscopes	49.5 (95–00)	Endoscopic/MIS
7	PTMR products	47.8 (00–04)	Cardiovascular
8	Bone growth substitutes and growth factors	47.0 (97–04)	Orthopedics
9	Growth factor dressings	46.0 (97–04)	Wound care
10	Vascular stent-grafts	46.0 (97–04)	Cardiovascular

Under this definition, devices might be considered as belonging to one of nine categories (North American industrial classification): surgical and medical instruments, ophthalmic, dental, lab apparatus, irradiation, specialty devices, medical/surgical supplies, *in vitro* diagnostics, and electromedical. There were (in 2000) 16 170 companies involved in these sectors – 6750 of them manufacturers worldwide. The US market is approximately $68 billion, or 48% of the annual global market (MDDI, 2000) (see Table 3.3).

The top 20 medical devices in terms of revenues in 1999 were the following:

1 Incontinence supplies
2 Home blood glucose-monitoring products
3 Wound closure products
4 Implantable defibrillators
5 Soft contact lenses
6 Orthopedic fixation devices
7 Pacemakers
8 Examination gloves
9 Interventional cardiovascular coronary stents
10 Arthroscopic accessory instruments
11 Prosthetic knee joint implants
12 Lens care products
13 Prosthetic hip joint implants
14 Multiparameter patient-monitoring equipment
15 Mechanical wound closure

16   Wound suture products
17   Absorbable polymers
18   Hearing aids
19   Wheelchair and scooter/mobility aids
20   Peritoneal dialysis sets

The steps and processes involved in developing and bringing to market a new medical device are significantly different than those in pharmaceutical development. This process, while less complex, less expensive, and shorter than that for a drug, is also less well defined and less profitable if successful. But the fundamental objectives in development and approval are the same as for a drug – to have a product that can be profitably marketed with proven therapeutic efficacy and safety.

There are two significant* routes to regulatory approval (and therefore development) for a device (Kahan, 2000). The 510(k) route is less rigorous but requires that the device be either Class II or III (the lower two categories of risk) and that there already be a similar ('predicate') device on the market. Such devices may or may not require clinical studies (efficacy and safety may be adequately established in nonclinical studies). Suitable materials must be utilized (and analytical data must be available to establish that the levels of purity and nature of impurities in said materials are acceptable), and the resulting actual product must be sterilized, packaged, and labeled in accordance with regulatory requirements. Also a 510(k) application must be assembled, submitted, and approved by CDRH. Such applications account for roughly 98% of new devices, with only 10% of such applications requiring clinical testing.

The other route for approval requires a PMA (pre-market approval). Devices coming to market by this regulatory route include all of those in Class I and also those in Class II that either do not have a predicate or are of some specified categories. Clinical studies must always be performed for these to both demonstrate efficacy and evaluate safety in clinical use.

BIOCOMPATIBILITY

The year 1990 saw the passage of the Safe Medical Devices Act, which made premarketing requirements and postmarketing surveillance more rigorous. The actual current guidelines for testing started with the USP guidance on biocompatibility of plastics. A formal regulatory approach springs from the

* Note: The 510(j) approval route is very rare and will not be discussed here.

Tripartite Agreement, which is a joint intergovernmental agreement between the United Kingdom, Canada, and the United States (with France having joined later). After lengthy consideration, the FDA has announced acceptance of International Standards Organization (ISO) 10993 guidelines for testing (ASTM, 1990; O'Grady, 1990; FAO, 1991; MAPI, 1992; Spizizen, 1992) under the rubric of harmonization. This is the second major trend operative in device regulation: the internationalization of the marketplace with accompanying efforts to harmonize regulations. Under the ICH (International Conference on Harmonization) great strides have been made in this area.

Independent of FDA initiatives, the USP has promulgated test methods and standards for various aspects of establishing the safety of drugs (e.g. the recent standards for inclusion of volatiles in formulated drug products), which were, in effect, regulations affecting the safety of drugs and devices. Most of the actual current guidelines for the conduct of nonclinical safety evaluations of medical devices have evolved from such quasi-agency actions [e.g. the USP's 1965 promulgation of biological tests for plastics and ongoing American National Standards Institute (ANSI) standard promulgation].

A medical device that is adequately designed for its intended use should be safe for that use. The device should not release any harmful substances into the patient that can lead to adverse effects. Some manufacturers believe that biocompatibility is sufficiently indicated if their devices are made of medical grade material or materials approved by the FDA as direct or indirect additives. The term medical grade does not have an accepted legal or regulatory definition and can be misleading without biocompatibility testing.

There is no universally accepted definition for biomaterial and biocompatibility, yet the manufacturer who ultimately markets a device will be required by the FDA to demonstrate biocompatibility of the product as part of the assurance of its safety and effectiveness. The manufacturer is responsible for understanding biocompatibility tests and selecting methods that best demonstrate the following:

- The lack of adverse biological response from the biomaterial.
- The absence of adverse effects on patients.

The diversity of the materials used, types of medical devices, intended uses, exposures, and potential harms present an enormous challenge to design and conduct well-defined biocompatibility testing programs. The experience gained in one application area is not necessarily transferable to another application. The same applies to different or sometimes slightly different (variable) materials. Biodegradation and interaction of materials complicates the issue.

Biocompatibility describes the state of a biomaterial within a physiological environment without the material adversely affecting the tissue or the tissue adversely affecting the material. Biocompatibility is a chemical and physical interaction between the material and the tissue and the biological response to these reactions.

Biocompatibility assays are used to predict and prevent adverse reactions and establish the absence of any harmful effects of the material. Such assays help to determine the potential risk that the material may pose to the patient. The proper use of biocompatibility tests can reject potentially harmful materials while permitting safe materials to be used for manufacturing the device.

Any biocompatibility statement is useful only when it is considered in the proper context. A statement such as 'polypropylene is biocompatible' lacks precision and can lead to misunderstanding. Any statement of biocompatibility should include information on the type of device, the intended conditions of use, the degree of patient contact, and the potential of the device to cause harm. Manufacturers should avoid using the term biocompatible without clearly identifying the environment in which it is used and any limitations on such use.

The need for biocompatibility testing and the extent of such testing that should be performed depends on numerous factors. These factors include the type of device, intended use, liability, degree of patient contact, nature of the components, and potential of the device to cause harm. There are no universal tests to satisfy all situations, and there is no single test that can predict biological performance of the material or device and reliably predict the safety of the device. The types and intended uses of medical devices determine the types and number of tests required to establish biocompatibility. Biological tests should be performed under conditions that stimulate the actual use of the product or material as closely as possible and should demonstrate the biocompatibility of a material or device for a specific intended use. These tests will be more extensive for a new material than for those materials that have an established history of long and safe uses.

All materials used in the manufacture of a medical device should be considered for an evaluation of their suitability for intended use. Consideration should always be given to the possibility of the release of toxic substances from the base materials, as well as any contaminants that might remain after the manufacturing process or sterilization. The extent of these investigations will vary, depending on previously known information (prior art) and initial screening tests.

FUNDAMENTALS OF BIOCOMPATIBILITY TESTS

Biocompatibility is generally demonstrated by tests utilizing toxicological principles that provide information on the potential toxicity of materials in the clinical application (Gad, 2002). Many classical toxicological tests, however, were developed for a pure chemical agent, and are not applicable to biocompatibility testing of materials. In addition, medical devices are an unusual test subject in toxicity testing. A biomaterial is a complex entity, and the material toxicity is mediated by both physical and chemical properties. Toxicity from biomaterial often comes from leachable components, and the chemical composition of a material is often not known. Toxicological information on the material and its chemical composition is seldom available, and the possible interactions among the components in any given biological test system are seldom known.

Biocompatibility should not be defined by a single test. It is highly unlikely that a single parameter will be able to ensure biocompatibility, therefore it is necessary to test as many biocompatibility parameters as appropriate. It is also important to test as many samples as possible, therefore suitable positive and negative controls should produce a standard response index for repeated tests.

Additionally, the use of exaggerated conditions, such as using higher dose ranges and longer contact durations or multiple insults that are many factors more severe than the actual use condition, is important. Adopting an acceptable clinical exposure level that is multiple factors below the lowest toxic level has been a general practice.

Most of the biocompatibility tests are short-term tests to establish acute toxicity. Data from these short-term tests should not be stretched to cover the areas in which no test results are available.

Biocompatibility testing should be designed to assess the potential adverse effects under actual use conditions or specific conditions close to the actual use conditions. The physical and biological data obtained from biocompatibility tests should be correlated to the device and its use. Accuracy, reproducibility, and interpretability of tests depend on the method and equipment used and the investigator's skill and experience.

There are several toxicological principles that the investigator must consider before planning biocompatibility testing programs. Biocompatibility depends on the tissue that contacts the device. For example, the requirements for a blood-contacting device would be different from those applicable to a urethral catheter. Also, the degree of biocompatibility assurance depends on the involvement and the duration of contact with the human body. Some materials, such as those used in orthopedic implants, are meant to last for a long period in the patient. In this case, a biocompatibility testing program needs to show that the implant does not adversely affect the body during the long period of use. The possibility of biodegradation of material or device should not be ignored. Biodegradation by the body can change an implant's safety and effectiveness. The leachables from plastic used during a hemodialysis procedure may be very low, but the patient who is dialyzed three times a week may be exposed to a total of several grams during his or her lifetime, therefore cumulative effects (chronicity) should be assessed.

Two materials having the same chemical composition but different physical characteristics may not induce the same biological response. Also, past biological experiences with seemingly identical materials have their limits, too. Toxicity may come from leachable components of the material due to differences in formulation and manufacturing procedures.

Empirical correlation between biocompatibility testing results and actual toxic findings in humans and the extrapolation of the quantitative results from short-term *in vitro* tests to quantitative toxicity at the time of use are controversial. These need careful and scientifically sound interpretation and adjustment. The control of variation in biological susceptibility and resistance to obtain a biological response range for toxic effect needs careful attention as do the host factors that determine the variability of susceptibility in toxicological response adjustment to susceptibility. Variability in the human populations also needs careful attention.

The challenge of biocompatibility is to create and use knowledge to reduce the degree of unknowns and to help make the best possible decisions. The hazard presented by a substance, with its inherent toxic potential, can only be manifested when fully exposed in a patient. Risk, which is actual or potential harm, is therefore a function of toxic hazard and exposure. The safety of any leachables contained in the device or on the surface can be evaluated by determining the total amount of potentially harmful substance, estimating the amount reaching the patient's tissues, assessing the risk of exposure, and performing the risk versus benefit analysis. Then the potential harm from the use of biomaterial is identified from the biocompatibility of an alternate material.

TABLE 3.4

Clinical grant spending for medical device trials

	US $ in millions
1994	100
1998	250
2002	530

CLINICAL TESTING

Current data indicate that large medical device developers are conducting fewer studies at fewer locations, but the sheer number of products in the pipeline is providing significant opportunities for investigative sites and CROs with experience conducting device trials. Indeed, spending on clinical medical device studies remains one of the fastest growing segments (Table 3.4). Whereas spending for clinical studies of drug therapies grew 14% annually over the past several years, spending for devices grew by more than 20% annually in that same period. It is estimated that sponsors will spend more than half a billion dollars on clinical research for medical device trials in 2002. Sponsor usage of CROs to manage device trials is also growing substantially. The driver of growth in medical device trials is not regulatory pressure, as is often the case. It is the medical community. 'Doctors are clearly the ones driving most of the research', said Charlie Whelan, an industry analyst in the medical device group of San Jose, California based Frost & Sullivan. 'They're conservative by nature and won't use something until they feel there's sufficient clinical evidence to support its use. Some doctors want more data than the FDA requires. They want longer-term data or want answers to more specific questions.'

Rapid growth in this market is expected to continue with physician demand for clinical trial evidence and a rich pipeline of new devices (Table 3.5). Although the number of original investigational device exemption (IDE) applications dropped slightly between 2000 and 2001, the number of pre-market approvals (PMAs) and PMA supplements have been increasing steadily. These devices are novel and present potentially higher risk. They also require more pre- and post-marketing clinical research studies. 'There is no shortage of opportunity in this market segment', said Whelan. 'Many hundreds of new device companies have been created in each of the past five years, fueled by an aging population and new technologies.'

TABLE 3.5

Original IDEs approved

	Number of IDEs
1991	220
1993	248
1995	210
1997	272
1999	305
2001	284

MARKET CHARACTERISTICS

The global medical device market, excluding imaging and clinical diagnostics, is now valued at over $150 billion annually. Product lines are numerous and diverse, ranging from latex gloves and wheelchairs to hearing aids and artificial hearts. About 80% of the medical device market is composed of small companies with fewer than 50 employees. Nearly one-quarter of the 13 000 + medical device and diagnostics manufacturers are start-up companies with no revenue. This fragmentation mirrors the multitude of small markets for a widely diverse range of devices used in medical interventions.

The strategy for most manufacturers is to get a 510(k), then do a clinical study. It's not an 'investigation device' anymore, and the FDA never sees the data. The studies are still subject to Part 56 and Part 50 regulations regarding IRB approval and informed consent, but the FDA is generally too busy with others things to ensure compliance.

Europe is again seeing a healthy portion of the activity, largely because devices are far less regulated across the Atlantic than in the US. The only regulatory strategy that makes sense is to do a clinical study in Europe and get approval first and then come to the US. Most often clinical trials are conducted in Europe where they tend to be larger projects with an average of 531 subjects per study versus 172 on average in the US. Companies specifically conduct five clinical studies to bring a device to market in Europe, more than twice the US average. Unlike the increasingly global nature of clinical trials for ethical pharmaceuticals, medical device trials are becoming less international.

Device companies are placing their studies in many of the same places where drug studies are conducted. Typically, clinical studies go to leading academic institutions where the prevalence of disease in the patient population is most representative.

TABLE 3.6

Increasing use of CROs for medical device trials

	Percentage of device companies who report using CRO for	
	1998	2001
Protocol design	0	11
CRF design	0	12
Monitoring services	13	29
Regulatory services	8	11
Statistical services	8	33

According to Frost & Sullivan, medical device companies contract out less than 5% of their clinical research projects to CROs (Table 3.6). 'They use CROs a lot less than drug companies', said Whelan. 'Our forecast suggests that, in coming years, the medical device industry is likely to outsource more of its R&D, but not very much – i.e. up to maybe 7% by 2005.' Most of the research that needs to be done can typically be done in-house. Doing research through a CRO also exposes the company to a lot of risk, including patent infringement. There are an estimated half dozen CROs in the US and another half dozen in Europe that cater mostly, if not exclusively, to medical device companies. Many of them are boutique CROs that specialize in particular types of devices. All of them are fairly small, with between five and 30 employees. The big, multi-purpose CROs, like Quintiles and Parexel, also assist sponsors with device trials. About 96% of medical device manufacturers utilize CROs, most frequently for statistical and monitoring services.

CHANGING FOCUS, CHANGING OVERSIGHT

The US device industry is continuously developing new and innovative techniques in areas such as molecular diagnostics (including tests for infectious diseases, inherited diseases, and cancer), minimally invasive surgery, biocompatible materials used for cardiovascular purposes, and orthopedic implants. Combination products, gene therapies, imaging technologies and devices that can be linked to bioterrorism are among the hottest areas of medical device research currently.

A recent report by Frost & Sullivan named digital radiography and molecular diagnostics as two sectors worth watching for new developments in the months ahead. As healthcare providers shift to digital radiography techniques,

TABLE 3.7

Improving development performance

	Percentage of IDEs approved by FDA in first review cycle
1997	69
1999	68
2001	80

image integration will gain in importance. The simulation will gain in importance. The simultaneous shift toward home healthcare and nursing-home care is also bound to spur demand – and thus the launch of new products – ranging from ambulatory aids to orthopedic supports. Products focusing on self-care, the geriatric population, and women are likely to experience impressive growth.

Regulations are as stringent for devices as for drugs, claim FDA officials (Table 3.7). Submission-to-decision review times, however, are now worse for original pre-market approvals (PMAs) than for new drug applications – 411 versus 365 days – and the highest since the passage of FDAMA. Review times on 501(k)s, meanwhile, are falling. Third-party review of eligible Class I and II 510(k) devices, paid for by the manufacturer, is a very small – but growing – contributor to review speed. The Center for Devices and Radiological Health's (CDRH's) Office of Device Evaluation (ODE) received only 107 510(k)s reviewed by third-party organizations in FY 2001, about 16% of all eligible 510(k), but that's a 128% increase over the 47 such submissions received the prior year. Expansion of the pilot program in March 2001 more than tripled the number of eligible devices to 670.

As the FDA itself reports, the frequency and consequence of hazards resulting from medical use error far exceed those arising from device failures. So the FDA is paying far more attention to device design and labeling. The Office of Health and Industry Programs (OHIP) assists CDRH's ODE by providing 'human factors reviews' for PMA and 510(k) devices. This included patient labeling reviews on 141 submissions to CDRH last year. The OHIP also issued a guidance document last year on medical device patient labeling, including a suggested sequence and content, and principles on the appearance of text and graphics.

Guidance has also been issued about when a device manufacturer may report changes or modifications to the clinical protocol in a five-day notice to the IRB as opposed to getting formal FDA approval. It clarifies the kind of protocol changes – i.e. modification of inclusion/exclusion criteria to define the target patient population better or increasing the frequency at which data are gathered – appropriate for the five-day notice provision. Other types of changes, such as to indication or type of study control, require prior approval.

The FDA has also posted for comment a proposed regulatory change that would require sponsors and investigators to inform the IRB of any prior IRB review of a proposed study. In the device world, companies do IRB shopping since the IRB makes the determination if the device poses significant or non-significant risk.

Device manufacturers share with pharmaceutical companies the headache of complying with the Health Insurance Portability and Accountability Act (HIPAA). In terms of sponsor access to source data, there must be statement of when authorization expires, such as until the PMA is approved or when the product is on the market. There should be a description of how far back in time the patient's medical records will need to be searched. The consent process should also include a statement that treatment, payment, and insurance reimbursement are not conditioned on signing. The document should specifically indicate information that will not be disclosed to the sponsor. And there should be a statement of when, and if, study data will be made available to study subjects. Even though the sponsor pays for a lab test, it becomes part of the patient's medical record. Patients have a right to see it unless they sign away that right during the consent process.

Under HIPAA, doctors will no longer have the right to look at the medical records of referred patients, even those within the same practice group. Investigators will need to go to the IRB to ask for a 'waiver of authorization'. That will add another two to three months to the timeline. The IRB must also get educated.

THE REVIEW SPEED PROBLEM

Device manufacturers have been pressuring the FDA to accelerate the review and approval cycle time. The average life span of a medical device is 18 months. It's not a question of the patent expiring. In 18 months, the product is obsolete. A competitor has a new bell or whistle that makes its product more desirable than yours.

In terms of review speed, FDAMA has done more to benefit pharmaceutical companies than device firms. Several manufacturers believe the FDA has recently slopped back into its old bad habits. With breakthrough technology, the FDA has a tendency to request information for 'educational purposes' that is not directly pertinent to determine the safety and effectiveness of the device in question.

A central problem at the FDA is a lack of resources to review the mandatory, more complicated studies. 'A growing number of premarket submissions are for medical technologies that pose novel review issues, like tissue-engineered products, hybrid technologies . . . and nanotechnology', according to industry trade group AdvaMed.

In 2001, the FDA received 70 PMA applications, the highest number in 10 years. CDRH alone reviews some 17 000 device submissions and inspects 15 000 manufacturers a year. Though it'll get a proposed $10 million budget increase in 2003, none of it is earmarked for device review. 'The FDA device program budget has remained essentially flat over the last 10 years, and has declined in real dollars after accounting for inflation', according to the AdvaMed report. 'In addition, staffing levels have declined 8% since 1995.' Limited resources have also prevented the FDA from offering up more device-specific guidance documents.

The FDA claims to be focusing on erasing hold-ups on PMA combination product reviews that often involve the expertise of 'a drug person, a materials person and an engineer', according to one CDRH official. 'The experts are all in-house, they're just not all in our center. And what's a priority for us is not necessarily a priority for anyone else.' In the past, the FDA has taken as long as 13 months simply to decide which agency – CDRH, the Center for Drug Evaluation and Research, or the Center for Biologics Evaluation and Research – should perform the review. In February, the FDA also established a combination products program to help deal with the delays. The FDA created a formal combination products office to assign products to the appropriate component of the FDA in 2003.

Mark Kramer, director of the program housed in the FDA's Office of the Ombudsman, said, 'Currently, we don't have an exact count on the number of combination products. And it's difficult to make a guess because a lot of these products don't require inter-center coordination and are reviewed entirely within one center that, over time, has developed certain expertise in that product area. Standard operating procedures are now under review by different centers within the FDA to make inter-agency reviews occur in a more organized and documented fashion.'

'The regulatory clock on the request for designation process used to determine which agency will review a combination product is 60 days', added Kramer. 'But at times submissions need to be supplemented with additional information, or companies request a meeting during the review period because they want to provide additional information. That can cause the total elapsed time to be over 60 days. However, we generally have an agreement with the sponsor to extend the review clock.'

Some FDA critics, meanwhile, believe approval times have become too short since FDAMA, and they fear that some manufacturers exacerbate the problem by doing as little testing as possible or by 'fudging' clinical data. A scathing July 29 article by *U.S. News & World Report* highlighted past regulatory violations of both Boston Scientific and Medtronic, including withholding important and known adverse events from the FDA. It also pointed out dangers inherent in the 510(k) process and under-funding an overburdened safety-monitoring agency. The FDA's Office of the Inspector General found that, between 1994 and 1999, regulatory violations were far from rare. Device trials were twice as likely as trials for drugs and biologics to violate FDA rules, including missing data, poor data collection, and falsification of data.

Several FDA information sheets have also been put out to offer a needed reminder to investigators and IRBs about the difference between 'significant risk' (SR) and 'nonsignificant risk' (NSR) device studies – i.e. extended wear contact lenses versus daily wear lenses. NSR device studies have fewer regulatory controls and don't require submission of an IDE application to the FDA. The IRB is supposed to make the SR or NSR determination but they have been known to forget FDA staff were given internal guidance in this area last fall.

Small device firms look for guidance and are respectful of clinical trial expertise once they find it. They are often idea-driven rather than market potential driven. The entire organization may consist of an engineer, head of regulatory and clinical affairs, and a receptionist. Many people in the medical device business are naïve and have little experience.

Unless and until something is done to increase FDA resources, review days on some of the most medically important devices will likely continue to rise. Congress is reportedly looking at an FDA reform package that would give the agency more money to implement process improvements. A program similar to the Prescription Drug User Fee Act is now being implemented for medical devices.

Like pharmaceuticals, there are multiple steps involved in developing a new medical device. Because the product lifecycle is shorter, the timelines for these steps are compressed. The phases can be considered to include:

- Prototype design.
- Vendor (to provide materials) selection and verification.

- Biocompatability and physical chemical evaluation.
- Clinical evaluation.
- Regulatory filing and approval.

Though the networks of contractors to support these steps are less extensive than those for pharmaceuticals, there are still a wide variety of sources and the management issues remain similar.

REFERENCES

ASTM (1990). *Standardization in Europe: A success story. ASTM Standardization News*, 38.

CDRH (1992). *Regulatory Requirements for Medical Devices: A Workshop Manual.* Center for Device and Radiological Health, HHS publication FDA 92-4165.

FAO (1991). Report of the FAO/WHO Conference on Food Standards, Chemicals in Food and Food Trade (in cooperation with GATT), Vol. 1, Rome, March 18–27.

GAD, S.C. (2002). *Safety Evaluation of Medical Devices*, 2nd edn. Marcel Dekker, New York.

KAHAN, J.S. (2000). *Medical Device Development: A Regulatory Overview.* Parexel, Waltham, MA.

MAPI (1992). The European Community's new approach to regulation of product standards and quality assurance (ISO 9000): What it means for US manufacturers. MAPI Economic Report ER-218.

MDDI (2000). Industry snapshot. *Med. Dev. Diag. Ind.*, December 47–56.

NUGENT, T.N. (1994). Health Care Products and Services Basic Analysis. Standard & Poor's Industry Surveys, New York.

O'GRADY, J. (1990). Interview with Charles M. Ludolph. *ASTM Standardization News*, 26.

SPIZIZEN, G. (1992). The ISO 9000 standards: Creating a level playing field for international quality. *Nat. Prod. Rev.*, Summer.

USP (2000). The United States Pharmacopoeia, XXIV § NF-19. US Pharmacopoeial Convention, Rockville, MD.

The Wilkerson Group (1999). Forces Reshaping the Performance and Contribution of the US Medical Device Industry. Health Industry Manufacturers Association, Washington, DC.

Functions and Types of CROs

The entire contract research/development and production industry is slowly coming into its own. The critical shortage of new drugs in the pipeline has forced a number of major pharmaceutical companies to form strategic partnerships with companies capable of bringing in resources not currently available in their own organizations. The dearth of new chemical entities and the pricing pressure from the managed care organizations and the state and federal governments has made every pharmaceutical company evaluate the costs of developing a new drug and commercial manufacturing. Most new drugs arise from small organizations which have very limited internal capabilities. At the same time, the limits of internal resources and increased regulatory requirements for bringing new products to market powers the same needs for the medical device industry.

There are two fundamental drivers for outsourcing in the pharmaceutical and medical device industries. The first is the need for access to sources of information, essential for the long-term success of any company. This has resulted in pharmaceutical companies buying up small innovative drug delivery and biotech companies, as their own laboratories run out of new drug molecules. The second major driver for outsourcing is the imperative to reduce the excessive costs and time in development that have developed within these industries. The push to reduce the costs and exploit the synergies that may come with partnerships has further led to an unprecedented rate of acquisitions and mergers within these industries for the last 12 years.

Pharmaceutical companies have always supported a thriving service sector, partly owing to the broad range of skills and technologies required to discover, develop, and manufacture a drug for the market. This has positioned these outsource organizations in the role of strategic partners. Types of CRO are listed in Table 4.1 with additional information in the Appendices.

TABLE 4.1

Types of CROs

	See Appendix
Nonclinical biological testing	
Pharmacology	B
Biocompatibility	A
In vitro screening	A, B
Toxicology	A
Metabolism	A, B
Pharmacokinetic modeling	B
Chemistry	
Medicinal chemistry	D
Synthesis	D
Active pharmaceutical ingredient (API) manufacture	D
Radiolabeled synthesis	C
Analytical method development/analysis	C
Bioanalytical method development/analysis	D
Biological product manufacturers	
Engineering	
Machine shops	B
Physical testing	B
Clinical	
Phase I centers	G
Clinical monitors	G
Statistical analysis	G
Site management organizations (SMOs)	G
Report writing services	G
Data management	G
Dosage forms	
Formulation development	E
Clinical test material (CTM) manufacturers	F
Labeling	F
Patient kit preparations	F
Pharmacy services	F
Contract sterilization	B
Regulatory	
IND preparation	H
NDA preparation	H
Annual update preparation	H
Regulatory advisors	H

HOLE IN THE VIRTUAL MODEL – GENERAL CONTRACTOR

A major (perhaps the major) problem with the virtual company pharmaceutical development model is that the proper placement monitoring, conduct and coordination of such efforts is complex and requires a level and range of skills which are rarely present in the virtual organization. A single individual or organization is needed to be able to act as a 'general contractor' for such activities. And such a service provider is all the better if they are experienced and able to provide some key services on their own.

Example: As an example of the complexity of outsourcing operations, contract formulation development should be considered.

The pharmaceutical industry is challenged by competitive pressures to shorten the new product development process. CROs have clearly demonstrated their ability to accelerate the pace of development in the clinical arena, where there are now myriad companies offering services in statistical analysis, clinical trials management, report writing, project management and bioanalytical testing (Parikh, 2001).

There is a growing trend in the industry to outsource product development, including such processes as formulation development, stability testing, manufacture of clinical trial supplies and the preparation of chemistry, manufacture and controls (CMC) documents.

Formulation development is a key area of product development patentability, lifecycle, and ultimately the success of a new product. Formulation development encompasses a very wide range of activities. Traditionally, formulation covers such functions as pre-formulation, including analytical assay development and characterization, excipient screening to stabilize or enhance the solubility of the product, and dosage form development, whether it involves a solid, liquid, topical, aerosol or other dosage form. Formulation development may also include assessing delivery options.

As advances in preclinical technology have generated a massive number of potential drug candidates, contract formulation development has become the only way for the industry to keep pace. There are essentially three reasons for companies of all sizes to choose to outsource their formulation development functions:

1 to compress timeline, i.e. reduce time to market;
2 to access a particular expertise, technology, facility or skill; and
3 to offset the risks of product failure.

The following issues must be considered for outsourcing any activity in general and formulations development in particular.

1 Determination of what needs to be outsourced.
2 Establishing the scope of the project.
3 Selection of an outsource partner.
4 Protection intellectual property.
5 Managing the project.

Determining outsourcing needs

The need to consider outsourcing formulation development is driven by various and unique internal factors within each company. These could include lack of skilled staff, no access to suitable equipment, time constraints and general lack of technological know-how. In short, the sponsor must decide if outsourcing is being considered for tactical reasons (contracting the project out because of time or manpower constraints) or strategic reasons (the sponsor does not have the technical resources in-house and has no intention of building them in-house).

The former situation is quite common among major pharmaceutical companies, where the number of projects far exceeds the available skilled manpower or the time allowed. The latter scenario tends to be found among virtual companies or small firms, where resources are at a distinct premium.

Nevertheless, the determination to outsource formulation development must be made with one clear understanding: the initial cost of going out-of-house will always be higher than doing the same project in-house. This fact always surprises companies when they consider outsourcing for the first time. This is understandable, for a number of companies the true cost of developing the product is complicated by the way the accounting department calculates the allocation of overhead costs.

Establishing the scope of the project

An integral part of formulation development is defining the ultimate clinical dosage form. In early development the dosage form is undefined. The decision often comes down to what is feasible, what is marketable and what is cost effective for a particular drug. Understanding the real goal of the project will redefine the selection criteria for selecting an outsource organization. Formulation development projects to be outsourced span a wide range of needs. An outsourced project may involve pre-formulation studies to clinical supply manufacturing or it may comprise a very limited sub-set of the development project.

A clearly defined list of essential activities and expectations must be established. The outsource organization must receive such information and key objectives such as the project budget, and schedule critical project milestones and deliverables in order to supply a request for proposal (RFP).

The scope of the project can be divided into pre-formulation development and formulation development. Normally some of the preliminary information may be available from the originating company and can be shared with the outsourcing organization. In most cases, the pre-formulation and formulation development is outsourced as a single project.

The requirements for different dosage forms are obviously different and must be identified. Some of the considerations are listed in Tables 4.2 and 4.3.

TABLE 4.2
Pre-formulation development research

---

(1) Active pharmaceutical ingredient (API) characterization
- Stability-indicating assay
- Purity (IR)
- Crystallization solvent
- Melting point
- % Volatiles
- Probable decay products
- Solubility profile, pK_a
- Physical properties (i.e. LOD, density, flow, particle size distribution, shape, surface area, etc.)
- Crystal properties and polymorphism
- Dissolution study, X-ray diffraction, IR analysis, thermal analysis, hot-stage microscopy
- Porosity (BET, mercury, etc.)
- Hygroscopicity
- Intrinsic dissolution

(2) Compatibility testing (i.e. excipients, components)

(3) Dosage form types

(4) API bulk stability

(5) Pre-formulation summary report

TABLE 4.3

Formulation development scope

(1) Pre-formulation development report review
(2) Chemical/physical stability
(3) Dissolution profile (if applicable)
(4) Bioavailability
(5) Formulation optimization
(6) Clinical evaluation

Selecting an outsource partner

As presented in Chapter 1, just as the pharmaceutical industry landscape is always changing with merging acquisitions and companies starting up or folding, so it is with the outsource service industry. The listings at the end of this book are certainly not globally complete, and will be out of date by the time they see print (as, by the way, are even some magazine advertisements for such companies). But I hope to have provided an excellent starting place for the selection process.

After the first round of selection, one should contact the remaining organizations and conduct the following actions:

1   Initiate confidentiality disclosure agreements (CDAs).
2   Study each outsourcer's literature.
3   Ask each outsource organization to fill out a 'Pre-visit questionnaire' to gain a more complete understanding of the organization, its response time and the degree of understanding that it may have about the type of project the sponsor wants to undertake. Some of the information to request in the questionnaire could include company name, location, facility description, equipment list history, organization chart, mission statement, financial report (for a public company), parent company information (if applicable), audit history, references, total number of employees, union or non-union workforce, industrial health and safety records, technical capabilities and a list of the company officers.
4   Once the pre-screening is complete, a quality audit needs to be initiated to observe further all the capabilities, and meet the people who will be managing the project. Find out what the workload on the formulation development staff is, how soon the project can be undertaken and whether the company can provide a tentative schedule for completion of certain

milestones. Answers to these questions will provide a good indication of the organization's technical and project management capabilities.

5   Discussing the reputation of the company with industry colleagues is another way of performing due diligence. These discussions can revolve around the quality of work, meeting of promised deadlines, reaction of the outsource organization when unexpected results were obtained, time between the completion of the project and the written reports, and any surprises in the final invoice for the services rendered.

Keep in mind, the plant visit is the most important step in selecting an outsourcing company.

If the scope of the project is beyond formulation development, such as process development, clinical supplies or manufacturing, it is advisable to evaluate the organization based on these anticipated outsourcing areas. If there is a remote possibility that you will need the outsource organization beyond the formulation development stage, you should consider the following:

- Experience in pharmaceutical development and manufacturing.
- Financial stability and liquidity.
- Production capacity at different levels.
- Current capacity utilization.
- How do they normally sign the commercial contracts? A normal commercial contract can be signed in several different ways:

    (i)   A 'cost plus' contract could require the contract manufacturer to reveal all of the operating costs and profits (open book) to the sponsor (not too many contractors are willing to do this).

    (ii) Another type of contract could be based on the 'spot price', which will mean that, when you want to manufacture your product, *if* the outsource organization has the time and capacity, they will entertain your business (this is not desirable if you want to have the assurance that the product will be available when you want it in the marketplace).

    (iii) The third type of contract is called 'take or pay', which guarantees the outsource organization certain yearly production volume and, in return, the sponsor reserves certain capacity to make sure the product will be available to sell. There may be other creative ways commercial contracts can be signed.

- How many commercial products are being manufactured at the current location?

6 Price and agreement reviews by the legal department for terms and conditions including the liabilities. It is advisable that you allow more than adequate time for the legal review, because it will always take longer than both parties think.

7 Clear responsibilities of each organization must be spelled out in the agreement. For example, if the pre-formulation work is done in your own or another organization and the development report indicates that the excipients are compatible, the outsource organization will complete the formulation development project based on that information. If that formulation shows a stability problem related to the compatibilities of the ingredients, the outsource organization should not be held responsible. There are a number of similarly unforeseen issues that may come up during the life of the project; each organization should have enough confidence in each other's professionalism that they can be resolved without too much problem.

Protecting intellectual property

When you are considering outsourcing, protecting you proprietary information is critical. Signing of the secrecy agreement alone should not be considered sufficient protection. Unless you are going to license specific technology for your product from the outsource organization, your agreement should specifically discuss who owns the outcome of the research if it involves some unique process or formulation technique, or yields unexpected positive results or product, etc.

Managing the project

Managing the project requires clear communication between the parties. Because formulation development is a relatively short-term project, the sponsor company can have a member of its staff, if possible, work alongside the outsource organization team at the critical juncture of the project.

Typically, detailed timelines and milestones are established. A check list may be advisable with clear responsibilities spelled out. The criteria for success are defined at the beginning of the project. This makes it easier to control and monitor the activities at the outsource organization. Monitoring such a project will give the sponsor a good understanding of the outsource organization's capabilities, people and business practices. This is a valuable assessment that will be beneficial if the sponsor company ever wants to consider the next step in the project, such as process development or commercial manufacturing of the product, if the outsource organization has those capabilities.

Pharmaceutical companies are in need of a method to grow their product pipelines in order to accelerate drug development and reach revenue demands. Outsourcing formulation development can provide new technology not available in house, besides compressing the time to market for a new drug. The processes of identifying the right outsource organization for a project may be streamlined by asking a series of questions internally, before seeking an outsourcing company.

A definitive project plan in terms of scope, timelines and deliverables will help the outsource organization provide appropriate cost estimates and time commitments. The due diligence after the selection of the organization must be carried out to avoid disappointments. Monitoring the project with clear milestones and proper oversight is of paramount importance for the success of the project.

REFERENCE

PARIKH, D. (2001). Formulation Development. *Contract Pharma*, October: 60–64.

Selection of CROs

The selection of service providers that outsourcing development activities require is a demanding activity. A successful development team will certainly include more than one provider, consisting of a group of specialist companies, individuals and organizations.

Despite the difficulties and new challenges this approach to R&D presents, data suggest that more and more companies – large and small – are implementing outsourcing programs as part of a strategy to accelerate the discovery process, control development costs, exploit profitable niche markets and minimize time to market. Indeed for small and mid-size companies, an outsource strategy is central from the beginning.

THE TREND TOWARDS OUTSOURCING

'Contracting out' or 'outsourcing' of chemical scale up and, more particularly, bulk manufacturing has always been an integral part of pharmaceutical industry activities, but outsourcing of biology is a more recent phenomenon. This is because the more mature industrial chemical industry was already using contract providers, a service that then became available for the younger pharmaceutical industry. The expense of investing in and maintaining chemical plant means that it must be fully utilized in order to maintain profitability; its use by a number of clients has obvious cost-saving elements. In the past, there existed neither the requirement nor the services necessary to consider outsourcing biological studies.

This changed in the early 1960s, when the tragedy of thalidomide revealed the importance of adverse toxicology and transformed the public policy surrounding drug safety. It was furthered by the introduction in 1977 of Good Laboratory Practice (GLP). Since these two events, the pharmaceutical industry has adapted outsourcing preclinical safety studies as an integral and essential part of their overall strategy. This can be similarly applied to the clinical work that is performed to supply proof of safety and efficacy of new drugs, and has been the norm for medical devices since the 1990 Safe Medical Device Act.

Outsourcing is now an essential element in the strategy of pharmaceutical companies. Far from being solely the province of large company strategy, outsourcing is used intensively by small companies aiming to adopt modern techniques in a flexible and competitive environment. Outsourcing can be taken to mean more than just contractual R&D, and can involve university and industrial collaborations. In the widest sense, outsourcing can range from contract R&D to acquisition, with a spectrum of joint ventures and research collaborations in between. Arrangements between parties can stretch from preferred provider contractual relationships, through to equity investments alongside research collaboration. For the purpose of this article, we'll narrow our definition of outsourcing to the contractual relationship between technology provider and client. This may involve a research or a development contract; however, the intellectual property in this definition remains with the sponsor, with payment based on completion of the sponsored work and not related to the ultimate success of the project.

RAPID GROWTH

In a recent report, outsourcing in the pharmaceutical industry was estimated as running about 80% of overall R&D spending (30% for large pharmaceutical companies), and rising (figures from Deutsche Banc Alex. Brown, Equity Research, Pharmaceutical Outsourcing 1999). Given that pharmaceutical R&D was estimated to run at more that $170 billion for the year 2000–1, this amounts to some $135 billion of expenditure annually. The overall outsourcing market is expected to grow significantly over time to perhaps 50% of pharmaceutical R&D for large pharmaceutical companies and 90% overall. In some areas such as outsourcing of chemistry-related functions the figure has recently been rising at a compound annual rate of 40–50%. Given the huge amounts of money spent on outsourcing it is perhaps surprising that more attention is not given to the procedures of selection.

This rather oligopolistic market representation should not disguise the fact that there is huge diversity amongst the smaller organizations not shown on the chart, and indeed, in the somewhat older manufacturing function, the split is much wider among a larger number of companies. In clinical and toxicological evaluation, many (though not all) of the tasks have similar skill requirement, and the generic nature of the processes involved tends to favor the agglomeration into larger business units. In chemical manufacture, there is a greater degree of specialization and a greater importance of specialized machinery and plant required to operate in different synthetic routes or in the manufacture of different formulations. However, it is also true that this segment of the outsourcing market is less mature than chemical manufacturing; this may also be a factor in the number of companies represented.

THE BUYING OF R&D

Management of outsourcing is a much more complex process than that of internal R&D. While the selling of R&D is a well-advanced process, the buying is not. Many companies incorrectly regard this as a normal extension of their in-house efforts with little training being given to those personnel who manage it. Frequently, they consider outsourcing as part of the purchasing function. The process of buying R&D can be divided into the following segments:

- The identification of potential providers.
- Selection of preferred providers.
- Negotiation of a contract.
- Management of the work.
- Receipt and utilization of the resulting product.

Identification of potential partners is itself a complex process, with more than 2000 companies in the business of offering contract pharmaceutical and medical device services. While there are 'for hire' directories of such organizations published (DIA, 2002; FDLI, 2002), only this volume covers the entire span of available resources.

Reflecting the complexity involved, a few of the larger CROs are offering a wider menu of services, in an effort to capture 'one-stop-shop' outsourcing. However, the risk for the buyer in choosing such offerings is that the quality value for money and coordination between groups is not always equally high. One is better served by selecting different companies with expertise particular to the service sought.

Selecting, planning and budgeting for the use of a CRO are critical to project success. CRO use continues to increase in the US and Europe and yet sponsors continue to encounter difficulties in these areas. Typical problems include:

- Insufficient knowledge of available providers.
- Finding the time and resources for evaluating and selecting a high-quality, experienced CRO.
- Unrealistic bid expectations.

73

- Poor bid specification leading to poor CRO performance.
- Difficulty comparing competing bids.
- An inability to specify rates and terms for any additional work on a basis comparable with the initial contract. This reflects the 'scope creep' problem faced by both the client and the provider.

SOURCES OF INFORMATION ON CROS

Identifying competent laboratories

The first step is to obtain a list of laboratories engaged in the contract provider field such as toxicological testing. Although other opportunities exist for obtaining such services, for example, university laboratories, laboratories of a consortium member's company, and, in some cases, government laboratories, the vast majority of externally placed studies involve the contracting party (the 'sponsor') placing a study in a 'contract laboratory'. Therefore, this situation will be used as the model for the rest of this chapter. The CRO (contract research organization) industry has become truly international, as is reflected in the lists provided in this volume. Laboratories can be selected based on a range of factors, as we shall see.

Published lists

Several lists of contract providers exist, but the most current available should be utilized. These lists are updated from time to time, since the contract laboratory industry is dynamic and the capabilities of an individual laboratory change over time. Also, it must be recognized that the contract research industry has become an international one, with services both provided and required by organizations in a large number of companies.

These compendia serve as a basic information for finding CROs capable of performing a specific task. More detailed information can be obtained by contacting (by phone, mail or email) the individual provider organizations.

Information available at meetings

A great deal of information about CROs can be obtained at scientific and industry meetings. Brochures which explain the types of services the CRO is capable of providing, and descriptions of facilities, staff, and price ranges for standard activities are displayed at such meetings by many contract service providers. Laboratory sales representatives (the current trend is to call these

'BD' or business development personnel) attend these meetings frequently to discuss specific study needs with prospective sponsors.

A second source of information available at meetings is the experience of professional colleagues, who may be able to provide advice on where to have certain kinds of services provided, having had similar work done previously. Of particular importance is information about where their work was done, its perceived quality, and how to avoid mistakes or misunderstandings in dealing with a particular contract laboratory.

This latter source of information needs to be taken with the proverbial 'grain of salt'. Almost anyone who has contracted R&D activities has had some problems; those who have contracted many projects have had at least one with a major problem; and probably every good contract provider has been inappropriately criticized for poor work at least once. A distorted evaluation is altogether possible if, for example, uncontrollable events (power shutdowns, shipping strikes, etc.) might have affected study results and the sponsor's overall impression of the provider.

For highly specialized work, choices in providers may be very limited. Phototoxicity testing, for example, is still a relative rarity. Reproductive and developmental toxicity evaluations, although offered by many laboratories, are tricky, demanding, and performed well by only a few. Inhalation toxicity testing is a similar case. An even more complex situation involves tests requiring several kinds of relatively unusual expertise or equipment. A developmental toxicity study which requires inhalation exposure, for example, may limit laboratory selection to only a few facilities. Contract providers will usually provide information on the availability of services in specialized areas, if they are unable to provide such testing themselves.

'Freedom of Information' requests

Copies of reports of laboratory inspections conducted by federal agencies are available under the Freedom of Information (FOI) Act and online at the FDA website. These reports generally follow the format of the laboratory inspection guidance given to Food and Drug Administration (FDA) investigators, and provide a great deal of information of varying utility. Since they are purged of references to proprietary activities, trademarks, specific sponsorship of studies, and much other information, it is sometimes difficult to understand the intent of the report. In addition, they present the opinions of individual investigators concerning isolated activities and events and therefore may not be truly representative of a laboratory's usual practices.

On the other hand, since the laboratory inspection procedures used by a particular agency are consistent, the FOI reports permit some comparison among laboratories. This information, coupled with other inputs, is therefore valuable and should not be ignored.

FOI requests should be made to the specific agency which conducted the inspection. Since the FDA's inspection program has been in existence for some time, they are the logical first agency to call in seeking inspection reports on particular laboratories.

Once a list of laboratories able to do the study in question has been drawn up, the most critical part of getting a good job done is in selecting *the* laboratory at which to place the study. The rest of this chapter will be spent reviewing selection criteria in detail.

This volume, of course, is intended to meet several unmet needs. A number of organizations provide interface between provider and client. These intermediaries provide a range of services, from information databases to consulting services, and in some cases even run studies themselves, acting as a sort of general contractor CRO.

Such companies offer more extensive information on CROs than pharma or biopharma companies tend to have in house, which allows savings on time and contract costs by facilitating charge comparison and negotiation of better CRO selection, thereby reducing the risk of selecting poorly qualified CROs. Mistakes in selection can be very costly both in terms of increased time to completion, project costs and poor performance, particularly where there may become a need for additional studies to make up for poorly conducted contracts. There are a number of independent consultants who also act as 'one-stop' CROs, arranging and coordinating all required activities for development. These usually handle only a few projects at a time (see www.toxconsultants.com or www.chemconsultants.com, for example).

DataEdge (www.dataedge.com) has collaborated with 30 larger pharmaceutical companies to define benchmarks and divide unit costs into 20 common budget categories, ranging from pre-trial regulatory filing to manuscript preparation. They prepared a unified process for CRO selection, which the company claims makes the preparation and evaluation of requirements for a proposal a much faster job. The CRO responds to a proposal involving detailed tasks described in familiar terminology. This all-inclusive proposal reduces initial and add-on costs by eliminating double charges. Preferred-provider rate can be readily compared with industry rates paid by other companies, and comparisons with other means of carrying out the work, such as using internal resources.

Similarly, Arachnova (www.arachnova.com) offers services in project leadership and outsourced project management, and provides a database (the Technology Web) with more than 1000 companies specifically in the CRO industry. Limited searching of the database is freely available via the BioPortfolio web portal at www.bioportfolio.com, but a CD-ROM version is available at a commercial rate.

A rather different model is employed by Inceutica (www.inceutica.com), founded in October 1999 to deliver web-enabled solutions for pharmaceutical/biotech R&D. Inceutica's technology platform aims to connect pharma and biopharma companies to service providers with the particular therapeutic expertise sought, regardless of geographical or organizational boundaries. The client company will post the request for proposal (RFP) form on the website, making it available for review by service vendors, allowing them to submit and revise project bids and selects the vendor that best fits their needs. Inceutica has no direct involvement in the two parties' communications.

Technomark (www.technomark.com) has provided a register of CROs since its conception in 1988. Initially focused on toxicology and clinical outsourcing, an addendum has recently been published which identifies contract pharmaceutical manufacturers and chemical synthesis companies. The information provided by the Technomark registers has also recently been enhanced by an on-line version of the database. As well as basic contact information, there are details on the finances and the number of staff in the CRO. This information is not provided for all CROs, and is particularly lacking from the small, often private entities, which make up the bulk (in number) of the service providers. While it is often said that it is the smaller private provider that is more financially exposed, the recent failure of Oread exemplifies the wide range of this business risk. It is interesting to compare the failed strategy of Oread, which was to become a fully fledged multidisciplinary development service provider, with that of Albany Molecular Research, which, while expanding its offerings, has nevertheless remained focused on chemical service provision.

A smaller version of the Technomark database is provided by InPharm (www.inpharm.com) in the FlexiPages part of the website. The information, which is given more in a directory format than a database, provides contact details for a wide range of agencies and suppliers serving the pharmaceutical and healthcare industries. The information is accessible for free on the web, and can be searched by keyword or browsed by category. There is little information on many of the featured companies, but some have a profile with more information. Although the total number of companies is around 1000, few are specifically in the contract pharmaceutical R&D field. From a business perspective, these data are funded by organizations paying for a profile to be included on the website. This has the advantage of being free to the user, but the disadvantages of being partial in scope and biased towards those that do pay for a profile. This is not the case with the information provided in the Appendices of this volume.

The middle tier

As with the client pharmaceutical and medical device companies themselves, the merger trends of recent years in pharmaceutical outsourcing could be seen as suggesting a future with ever fewer, ever larger providers. While there has remained room for niche CROs, there is a trend to provide a wide range of pharmaceutical development resources to optimize the drug development services in one organization. The real business challenge from such reorganization is to use this very large development resource to optimize the drug development process for the benefit of the pharmaceutical industry. As in any industry sector, integrating the activities of a large CRO organization, particularly one that has recently merged, has been a substantial internal challenge.

This trend has now been countered by the emergence of a new tier of company between the sponsor and the CRO, with the outsourced management of clinical trials through site management organizations (SMOs) as an example. SMOs provide CROs with physicians and coordinators to enable clinical research coordination and monitoring of phase II, III, and IV clinical trials. The SMO often has a number of therapeutic specialties and access to a large and diverse patient population for inclusion in the proposed research. In addition, SMOs usually employ full-time certified clinical research personnel for trial documentation and case report form completion. SMOs are judged by their ability to enroll patients in studies and start and complete a clinical drug trial in a timely manner. In essence, therefore, SMOs aim to streamline the functions of CROs and operate between the CRO and the investigator.

Unless and until the cost savings and efficiencies promised by the continuing round of CRO mergers can be realized, there will remain room for such intermediate size organizations, which can operate in a highly flexible sense to add value to the outsourcing process in pharmaceutical R&D.

The CRO business is highly competitive and in this respect it is similar to the product-based industry it serves. However, there is a major difference in the way the two industries compete for business. The pharmaceutical industry can hope to differentiate its products very clearly based on hard data obtained from efficacy, safety and pharmacoeconomic studies. Even in today's new healthcare environment, the market place is less price sensitive when clear clinical evidence for product advantage can be shown. This is in marked contrast to the CRO industry, which has an ever-shrinking number of large well-founded mature customers and a vast and expanding pool of young, small, and venture capital hungry customers. Differentiating and selling technical services to senior R&D management is very different from marketing products to doctors and healthcare providers. Claims that work can be completed faster, error free and reported to agreed timelines are generally not credible to customers: because all CROs make these claims.

The real added value that an individual company might bring in its service offerings needs to be more carefully considered. Given that the facilities, GLP/GMP/GCP status, and technical competence and the like are mostly undifferentiated for the successful CRO, the simple answer has to be knowledge and experience, that is, the technical and scientific complexity of the pharmaceutical and medical device development process. CROs that can capture this knowledge by employing professionally experienced leaders who can then cultivate the scientific culture of pharmaceutical development into their organization will be the winners of the fight to capture increased market share in a generally mature or shrinking market. Such people-based elements last only as long as these individuals are employed by the organization. Knowing the good and bad elements comes from experience of working relationships; expertise in one area does not imply talent in all areas. In some cases, specific technologies might add a further element of uniqueness, for example inhalation technology, continuous infusion technology, telemetry and transgenics.

There is increasing recognition that specialist companies can add value to the outsourcing process and many now see the role of an intermediary organization as beneficial to serving the research-based pharmaceutical sector. Indeed we should not be surprised. The word 'entrepreneur' literally means 'to take between': in all industries, as they mature and become more integrated, companies often become more specialist in their offerings and opportunities can open up for new commercial intermediaries. A useful comparator here is the computer manufacture industry, which is highly fragmented and based on outsourced networks. A final validation of this concept comes from the large CROs themselves, which, in order to offer the one-stop shop from which they can benefit substantially as a provider, often resort themselves to sub-contracting. It will be interesting to see how this trend develops in the next few years, in an age when the business of pharmaceutical development is still growing, becoming ever more international in scope, more competitive and more complex.

Outsourcing is no doubt a trend that will continue to expand and, in order to improve its efficiency, the ways in which it is managed are likely to see dramatic evolve.

Key considerations in selecting a lab

Dependability

By far the most important should be confidence that the contractor will per-form as agreed to (on time, on budget, honestly and delivering the agreed product) and will inform the client or their agent of problems and issues as they arise. For in longer projects such unexpected occurrences will occur, and are most likely and easily solved or addressed if attended to early.

Experience (activity or study type specific)

Unless a study or activity is very unusual, any CRO selected to perform it must be able to demonstrate that they have previously performed the desired type of work in a successful manner. If the desired work is unique or of an unusual nature, the CROs wishing to provide the service should produce a plan for 'refresher' training or performing a 'pilot study' so as to maximize the chances of success.

Does the laboratory employ personnel trained in the needed specialty? What about ancillary expertise (pathology, statistics)? If not directly employed by the laboratory, are trained specialists available on a consulting basis? For example, if the major emphasis of a study is the determination of the inhala-tion toxicity of a test agent, but a minor component concerns teratogenic effects, the selected laboratory will require skilled, experienced inhalation toxicologists on staff. The laboratory does not necessarily have to employ its own teratologists, however, since coverage of these evaluations may reason-ably be effected by consultants in this specialty.

A skilled, competent staff will be necessary to the conduct of the work. Pro-spective laboratories' personnel environments should be scrutinized for signs of frequent or rapid staff turnover, difficulties in recruiting and retaining new staff, and lack of career pathways for staff currently employed.

Many laboratories rely on independent organization certification to demonstrate a standard of achievement and competence on the part of their technical and scientific staff. For example, both the American Board of Toxicology (ABT) and the Academy of Toxicologic Sciences (ATS) have certification programs for toxicologists. Likewise, the American Association of Laboratory Animal Sciences (AALAS) has three stages for certification of laboratory animal technical staff. Other specialties have similar certification programs based on some combination of experience and achievement demonstrated by written and practical testing.

Hand in hand with personnel availability is the selection criterion of technical expertise. Many different specialties are brought to bear on a particular study. The more complex the study, the greater the difficulty in finding a contract laboratory with all the necessary expertise.

In attempting to evaluate the qualifications of contract laboratory staff, organizational charts and curricula vitae should be obtained. These documents are standard tools which are used by contract laboratories as marketing aids. The FDA's Good Laboratory Practice (GLP) regulations require laboratories to maintain documentation of the training, experience and job descriptions of personnel. This is usually done by means of compilations of curricula vitae.

Another important point in evaluating staff capabilities is the number of people employed by the laboratory. The proposed study staff should be sufficient to perform all the work required. Attention should be directed to the laboratory's overall workload relative to available staff.

Equipment

Are all of the required instruments, tools, supplies, reagents, computer and such in place, operational, properly maintained and calibrated and labeled? Are the knowledge and skills of senior scientific staff suitable to the required works? Do they have prior experience performing such works? Are the actual technicians who will be performing the day-to-day works suitable? What is the turnover rate for the staff at the facility?

Cost

As a general rule, all contract research and development should be put out for bid by several CROs (but not too many – such bids take work to prepare, and it is unfair to ask for such if there is not a good chance that a contract will be awarded). Care should be exercised to provide sufficient information and detail to the potential bidders to ensure that they all end up rendering bids on the same work.

Facilities

Are the facilities (buildings, rooms, and environmental support services such as water, heat, air, and power) sound, well maintained, suitably monitored, sufficient to the tasks and clean? Particularly if living organisms are involved, it is essential that provisions for any power failures (that is, back-up generators) be present.

Laboratory animal care facilities may be accredited by the American Association for Accreditation of Laboratory Animal Care (AAALAC). This is a voluntary body which accredits laboratories based on its own standards as supplemented and reinforced by those of other organizations. Accreditation is based on elements of several major activities, programs or capabilities of the individual laboratory, such as veterinary resources, physical resources, administrative matters and the presence and activity of an animal care and use (animal welfare) committee. AAALAC accreditation is frequently the only objective symbol of the general compliance of the laboratory with standards of good practice in animal use and care, veterinary, physical plant, and administrative areas. Although no guarantee that the laboratory does good testing, AAALAC accreditation represents a worthwhile first step toward excellence.

Regulatory history

Regulatory agencies remember both good and bad performances by regulated contractors. They regularly audit such and the results of these audits are public records which should be provided upon request by the contractor and which are available online from FDA.

A large portion of the initial visit to prospective contract laboratories can usefully be spent in reviewing standard operating procedures (SOPs). These should be written for all routinely performed activities.

GLPs require that SOPs be established in the following general areas: animal room preparation, animal care, test and control substance management, test system (animal) observations, laboratory tests, management of on-study dead or moribund animals, necropsy, specimen collection and identification, histopathology, data management, equipment maintenance and calibration, identification of animals, and quality assurance. Although not specifically required by GLP regulations, the laboratory should also have SOPs for archiving activities. In each of these areas, numerous individual SOPs should be in place. For example, in the area of histopathology, SOPs should be available to describe tissue selection, preparation, processing, staining, and coverslipping; slide labeling and packaging; and storage and retention of wet tissues, blocks, and slides. Similarly, SOPs should be available for maintenance and calibration of all equipment and instrumentation which requires these activities.

The laboratory's SOPs should be clear, understandable, and sufficiently detailed to permit a technically experienced person to perform them. They should be up to date, and the method for keeping them current should be described. They should have the sanction of facility management, usually provided by signature of the person responsible for the pertinent laboratory activity.

To be effective, SOPs should be available to those who need them. For example, animal care SOPs should be available to vivarium workers, as analytical and clinical chemistry SOPs should be available in these laboratories. Compendia of SOPs which sit pristinely on shelves in offices may not reflect what is actually occurring in the laboratories and animal quarters. Likewise, SOPs which have not been reviewed or revised in several years should be viewed with suspicion. Improvement in actual methods occur frequently, and should be reflected in the written procedures.

If the laboratory has contracts with other laboratories, SOPs should be available for the secondary laboratories as well. Both the SOPs and these contracts should be reviewed in the same way.

Computerization

The days when all but a minority of data and records are recorded, captured and manipulated by hand are gone. The degree and quality of automation and computer resources of a potential contractor must be assessed as should the overall integration of such systems and plans and progress towards Section II GLP compliance.

Financial soundness

In Chapter 1 a list of extinct laboratories was provided. Several of these ceased operations with studies in progress and without notifying sponsors in advance owing to financial failure. To avoid this, one needs to assess the financial ability of a contract organization to continue operations and complete works. For many contractors, Dunn and Bradsturely can provide such information.

Location

Much is sometimes made (frequently by competitors in a negative way) as to the importance of location of facilities. While there are some factors which are related to location which should be considered (ease of travel and perhaps travel cost, stability and availability of technical staff, and security come to mind), the author's belief is this is near the bottom.

A consideration in selection of contract laboratories is the sponsor's ease of monitoring the study, which is largely a function of distance between the sponsor and the laboratory. In some studies, this may be a major consideration; in others, not worthy of mention. If the study is complex and requires frequent oversight, a trade-off may need to be made between the best laboratory relative to the previously mentioned selection criteria and monitoring ease.

On the other hand, sponsors do not plan complex studies unless they anticipate substantial product safety evaluation concerns, and therefore, considerable potential profit. If this is the case, the relatively small additional sum spent in the increased cost of frequent or distant monitoring may be minuscule in the eyes of those selecting the laboratory.

Site visits of prospective contract laboratories

In scheduling site visits with contract laboratories, the objectives should be clearly defined. Meeting those people who will be directing and contributing importantly to the study provides an opportunity to evaluate their understanding of the nature of the questions or problems which may arise. Ancillary contributors (pathologists, statisticians) should be interviewed carefully as well, since their contributions can be of fundamental significance to the quality and outcome of the study.

The facilities should be toured, looking for appropriate size, construction, spacing and design. GLP regulations as promulgated under the Food, Drug and Cosmetic Act, the Toxic Substances Control Act, or the Federal Insecticide, Fungicide and Rodenticide Act provide guidance as to the general facility, equipment and operational requirements of laboratories.

Storage areas for extra racks and cages, feed and bedding, and so forth are frequently inadequate in laboratories, and these facilities should be inspected and evaluated.

The FDA provides their field investigators who conduct laboratory inspections for compliance with GLPs with 'Compliance Guidance Manuals'. These are comprehensive documents which use a checklist approach to inspecting a laboratory for adherence to all the elements of GLP regulations. They can be obtained from the agencies, and can be used as guidance for study sponsors in evaluating prospective laboratories. An advantage of using this approach is that the sponsor will not omit an important element in inspecting a prospective laboratory. However, the sponsor should not get so bogged down in reviewing checklist items that actual observation of the laboratory is abbreviated.

Once an initial review of potential service providers has been conducted, those that remain in consideration (no more than three is a suggested limit) should be visited for on-site qualification. Table 5.1 below (with CVs provided) provides a sample agenda for such a visit.

Cost

A key factor in laboratory selection for most sponsors is the cost of the study. This single element can largely affect the quality of a study. 'Caveat emptor' applies equally to the toxicologist as to the home consumer. Many of the negotiable elements of a carefully defined study will not be performed in a similarly titled study at a different laboratory for a lower cost. Conversely, some of the extras offered for a higher priced study should not be included for extra cost if they are neither necessary nor desirable. The objective in considering the cost of a study is to select the laboratory which offers all the essential study elements at the lowest cost consistent with good quality. Good quality in turn relies on the other criteria previously discussed. When a laboratory is found which can perform all desired elements of the study, does high quality work, and offers a lower price for the study than its competitors, this is probably the laboratory to choose to perform the study.

In discussing costs, the sponsor should attempt to determine whether the laboratory will be able to add elements to the study if this appears desirable as the study progresses. The laboratory should have the capability to expand the original study design. Sponsor and laboratory should attempt to foresee how the cost of such additions would be determined.

Reputation

The reputation held by particular contract laboratories is clearly a guide in laboratory selection. Although not an absolutely reliable indicator of the worth of a contract laboratory's efforts, by and large laboratories earn their

TABLE 5.1

Sample agenda for a qualification visit to a CRO

Global presentation by the CRO/vendor
- Range of services offered.
- Company history.
- Organizational chart of the company.
- Presentation of potential study team.
- Previous experience and references.
- Number and type of ongoing/future projects.
- Previous audits.

Tour of the facility
Project management
- Discuss interfaces/coordination with CRO and sponsor, project team structure and reporting processes (including review of staffing estimate, CVs, training plan/ records, job descriptions).
- Discuss logistics/process review and project team coordination (including data flow, data transmission capabilities, reconciliation with other databases, management of committees, samples of timelines, quality controls, problem identification and resolution processes).

Data management
- Demonstration of the data management system (data entry, data query system, tracking of CRFs, tracking of queries, process flow chart, standard metrics, e.g. time from last subject out to database lock).
- Demonstration of the central randomization system.
- Review drug distribution capabilities and interface with the central randomization system.
- Review data management and central randomization system validation documentation.
- Review procedures for reconciliation with other databases.
- Review manual vs. automated processes and validations.
- Discuss ability to use sponsor coding dictionaries.

Quality assurance
- Review CRO organizational structure (organizational charts, mission/quality statement, training records, training policy).
- Review QA department activities, reporting relationships, quality manual, quality records, and QA SOPs/standards.
- Review reference files management (regulatory documentation/guidelines).
- Review SOPs.
- Review quality controls and audits.
- Review equipment inventory.

Wrap-up/summary of findings (sponsor)
- Present and discuss any finding from SOPs or other departmental review.
- Determine need for additional qualification data or visits by additional sponsor personnel.
- Establish plan for CRO to provide any missing data identified during visit.
- Schedule a mutually acceptable time for presentation of the formal report of the sponsor's findings. During this meeting the CRO will need to be ready to create a plan to address and 'deficiencies' found during the visit.

---

reputations over time. Beware of laboratories which submit low bids for studies and either cut corners to stay within their quoted cost or include add-ons, at the sponsor's expense, through the course of the study. Study additions can significantly increase the actual cost if the contract requires the sponsor to pay for them.

Other laboratories try to foresee likely additional aspects of the study, which may increase the quoted cost but yield a much better product. Producing the study at the price quoted is only one part of a contract laboratory's reputation. Quality, professional qualifications of staff, activity in scientific professional societies, accreditation, regulatory interface, and many other issues are important as well.

Protection of client confidentiality

Most contract laboratories expend considerable effort in trying to maintain confidentiality on behalf of their clients. In walking through a laboratory, clients should not be able to see proprietary labels on test material containers, or cage labels which state company names. A contract laboratory concerned about client confidentiality will be careful not to allow visible evidence to be seen by other potential clients. Confidentiality is usually of significant concern and should be discussed with laboratory management. The laboratory's master schedule should maintain client confidentiality as well.

Prior experience

Prior experience with specific contract laboratories simplifies the task of selecting a laboratory. Establishing a continuing relationship with one or several laboratories in the case of routine testing provides an opportunity to fine-tune study protocols. This will be discussed in greater detail below.

Scheduling

Undoubtedly, starting the study as soon as possible is important. The ability of the laboratory to begin the study soon may well determine where the study is performed. Most of the larger contract houses can start all but very large studies within 4–6 weeks. Some studies may be able to be initiated on even shorter notice. Certainly for shorter studies, less complicated protocols are needed and generally less lead time is required to begin the study. The converse is equally true, so if the study is large, long-term, or complicated, a fairly long time before study initiation will be needed to get the details of the study worked out with the laboratory. As a result, a laboratory which is willing to start a lengthy or complex study before the details have been settled should generally be avoided.

Special capabilities

As the science of toxicology and the questions society, regulatory agencies, and companies seek to answer become more complex, technical skills and equipment which are not widely available become more in demand. Such special capabilities are frequently resident in smaller or university laboratories where procedures, documentation, and adherence to regulatory standards may not be as rigorous as either one's own corporation or larger contract laboratories. One may even have to help investigators develop protocols, standard operating procedures, and record-keeping systems. Evaluating technical competency for specialized procedures is obviously difficult, as one is usually dependent on others to identify such specialists initially and they may also have to get outside help to evaluate the appropriateness and quality of the results. A not uncommon case of special capabilities is when human testing (such as repeat insult patch testing, or RIPT, must be performed). Here one must understand the special regulatory, legal, and ethical strictures on work with human subjects, and generally deal with an IRB (institutional review board) which must review, approve, and oversee any such human studies from the perspective of subject protection and ethics.

The contract

General terms of the contract should address such aspects as timeliness, proprietary rights, confidentiality, adherence to regulatory requirements (in the research effort and in the laboratory's practices in waste disposal, workers' protection, and safety, etc.), type and frequency of reports, communications between parties, conditions under which the study may be aborted and restarted, timing and method of payment, and the like. Such a contract '... should be negotiated by a team of lawyers and scientists who have a thorough understanding of the problems to be investigated, including both the scientific issues and the potential business implications ... Armed with this ... understanding, the lawyers can then proceed to develop a contract that is appropriate to the situation. ... Much of the language will be routine or "boiler plate" the type commonly found in agreements of various kinds'. (*Source*: Dr Edward Gralla, personal communication)

The contract should specify who does what in the furtherance of the study. For example, if analysis is necessary, the sponsor may wish to retain the responsibility to analyze the test material as a means of keeping its identity confidential. The derivative concern about documentation of the analysis is presumably also retained by the sponsor, but the contract should be clear on the responsibilities of both parties.

When discussing study personnel, various degrees of authority are vested in contract laboratory study staff by the sponsor. The study contract should define as clearly as possible the degree of authority vested in the contract laboratory staff and at what point the sponsor would be consulted for a decision when unforeseen situations arise. In general terms, then, the contract should define the rights and responsibilities of both parties.

The contract should also address financial matters, such as the cost of the study and the method and timing of payment. Certain unanticipated activities not directly related to the study may increase the cost to the laboratory; the contract should attempt to anticipate these events and establish reasonable incremental costs to the sponsor to deal with them. For example, study-specific inspections by agencies authorized to review a study (FDA or EPA) may add to the cost to the laboratory for additional staff time to accompany inspectors, copy documents, and otherwise field the inspections. If the sponsor wishes to be present at such inspections, additional direct costs will be incurred. Although many readers would view this simply as part of the laboratory's cost of doing business, the contract should anticipate how each party is expected to respond financially if the inspection becomes very time-consuming or onerous.

Likewise, post-study activities and responsibilities should be defined in the contract. Who will archive tissue and other samples and specimens? For how long? If statistical analysis is to be performed, of what does it consist? Who decides? If further analysis appears desirable after evaluation of the data, will the sponsor incur extra costs?

The study protocol

The most important part of site visits to laboratories will be the discussion of the study and establishment of the protocol. Extensive prior experience of the sponsor in conducting the contemplated study is helpful although many elements may still have to be negotiated. If the sponsor has limited experience, the importance of the protocol increases, since it contains the specific language of the contract between sponsor and laboratory which governs the conduct of the study.

To write a protocol with little flexibility may preclude the study director's judgment and may actually compromise the quality of the study. Each party must feel comfortable that the study protocol provides sufficient detail to specify what is to be done, when, and under what conditions. However, the protocol must not be so rigid that the study director is hampered in responding to changing conditions and events as they occur. Since unanticipated events almost always occur, the objective is to provide a protocol which permits the study to be conducted as closely as possible to the original study plan and to answer all the important study questions.

Other terms

Authorship

The question of authorship of publications resulting from the proposed study should be covered in the contract. Not all work is worthy of publication nor do contract laboratory staff often get an opportunity to author papers. But if the laboratory has contributed significantly to the work, and a publication is contemplated, help in writing portions of the manuscript should be solicited from members of the study staff, for which coauthorship is a deserved award.

Reports

The contract should specify the nature and frequency of reports which the laboratory will make to the sponsor. For example, a short-term study (two weeks or less) may require only telephone confirmation of study start, status of the animals at the halfway point, confirmation of termination, and the usual draft and final report.

For a longer study, the sponsor may request written status reports at regular intervals. In the case of chronic studies the sponsor may wish to have formal interim reports prepared by the laboratory. The contract should clearly specify the expectations of both parties concerning reports.

Inspections by the sponsor

Most contract laboratories do not like the thought of unscheduled site visits by study sponsors, for understandable reasons. Under ordinary circumstances, a large amount of staff time is spent escorting visitors through the laboratory. Unscheduled visitors therefore place an additional burden on already stretched resources.

Nevertheless, the right to monitor study progress at any reasonable time should be explicitly affirmed in the contract. This right, although perhaps never exercised by the sponsor, should not be relinquished. As a practical matter, unscheduled monitoring visits almost never occur, since the sponsor must recognize that the study staff may be unavailable at the time of the visit, making the trip a wasted one.

Likewise, the contract should explicitly grant the sponsor access to the laboratory's quality assurance (QA) inspection reports of the study. These reports are ordinarily *not* available to government investigators, and some contract laboratories prefer not to share them. However, a sponsor should ensure that the contract grants access to the QA reports.

REFERENCES

DIA (2003). *Contract Service Organization Directory*. Drug Information Association, Fort Washington, PA.

FDLI (2003). *Directory of Lawyers and Consultants*. FDLI, Washington, DC.

GRALLA, E.J. (ed.) (1981). *Scientific Considerations in Monitoring and Evaluating Toxicological Research*. Hemisphere Publishing Corporation, Washington, DC.

Contracting, Pricing, and Cost of Works Performed by CROs

Once a source is selected to perform work under contract, a great deal of effort still remains for the sponsor or sponsor's agent before work is actually initiated, and more still before the desired product is in hand. At the front of this process is the development of a contract that ensures that desired work will be done and that the final product will meet your needs.

As a starting place, consider a few 'rules' that any contractor should adhere to. A vendor or consultant should:

1   Provide realistic costs, dates, and number estimates to the client or potential client.
2   Do whatever is possible to establish and maintain a positive, open, and honest relationship with each client.
3   Be proactive about providing information and suggestions to help a client enhance the quality or speed of their work.
4   Appoint a primary contact person to interact with each client.
5   Do whatever is necessary to meet one's time and cost commitments.
6   Provide the highest quality product possible given the time and cost constraints.
7   Provide all services required and be willing to go beyond the strict limits of the contract to ensure the client is pleased with the services.

With these in mind, careful consideration can now be given to key areas.

COSTING

Probably the first component of a contract to be addressed is the costing of the work. Indeed (as presented in Chapter 5) this is almost always a consideration in the process of vendor selection. But the need to be clear and precise in what is expected from a contractor does not end with the selection of same in the bidding process. From this point an agreement and/or contract must be developed. If a protocol is involved, it should also be considered part of the specifications of work.

Social concerns over the growing impact of technology on our environment and our ultimate well-being has erupted into positive political action leading to a new array of laws and regulations. This of course is a bonanza for lawyers, who in customary unbeloved fashion, have proceeded to establish themselves as indispensable participants in defining and resolving new fields of conflict. Quite obviously, it is also a bonanza for bureaucrats, who have inherited a Solomon's mine of new power and jurisdiction from which they have already produced considerable gold plated gobbledygook along with a veritable waste dump of semantic slag.

But lawyers and bureaucrats have not been the only ones to find prosperity in these new laws. Surely there has never been a brighter time for toxicologists and other scientific professionals, to whom we must all look for answers to so many questions and whose services are therefore in such enormous demand.

Some people continue to battle what they regard the 'nonproductive nature' of all this activity and expense, even while reluctantly accepting it as a fact of contemporary business life. Certainly the impact of the environmental era is making it harder for some businesses to make money, at least over the short run. Certainly the additional costs of regulatory requirements add to the ultimate cost of goods and are aggravating our vexatious inflation problems. Certainly the social cost is compounded by the huge new bureaucracies that this movement has fostered. But a purely materialistic balance-sheet concept of productivity seems far too narrow. If productivity is defined more generously to include the objective improvement of everyone's health and safety, then the great surge of concern over health and the potential hazards of drugs is very productive indeed.

In all events, it is clear that lawyers and scientists must learn to deal productively with each other if the problems of the environmental era are to be resolved productively for everyone. This means that they must understand each other. In the interest of such understanding, and before passing to a discussion of some practical legal issues, it will be useful to mention one dichotomy that frequently gives rise to confusion, failure of communication, and sometimes outright antagonism between lawyers and scientists. I am referring to the difference between 'scientific fact' and 'legal fact'.

This dichotomy arises from the different basic objectives of the two disciplines. The objective of science is the pursuit of knowledge about the physical world in all its attributes. The objective of law, however, is the minimization and resolution of disputes. To the scientist, a 'fact' is a particular aspect of objective reality; to the lawyer, a 'fact' is simply a state of knowledge that is adequate to support the interest of the client in a particular dispute. For example, toxicologists are extremely interested in the mechanism of genetic mutation as an element in understanding the biochemistry of carcinogenesis. They want to know objectively whether a single dose of a new drug can induce a cancer or whether the mechanism requires some threshold concentration. The question has enormous practical consequences, but scientists are fundamentally interested in finding out the truth, regardless of consequence. The lawyer is also interested in scientific truth, but will seldom be objective about it. If the businessmen and clients of a pharmaceutical manufacturer would be wiped out by a 'zero tolerance' rule, the lawyer will try to persuade the court or agency that there is in fact a 'no-effect' level within which the client should be allowed to operate. Representing a 'class' of possible injured patients who would like to see the factory drug taken off the market, the lawyer will argue that the single-molecule concept is in fact correct. If doubt must be conceded, the lawyer will still argue that the theory most congenial to his of her client's interest is the more likely. In short, there would be no hesitation to build arguments in support of the client's desired conclusion and to ignore or explain away any contrary views, which is the very opposite of the scientific method. Furthermore, if the trend of objective scientific research seems to be running against the argument, the lawyer will often mount a rearguard action to postpone as long as possible the legal recognition and acceptance of this adverse scientific reality.

Of course, this is an unfair oversimplification of the lawyer's role. In practice there are ethical constraints on the lengths to which counsel may go in advocating the client's cause, and sophisticated clients will seldom want their lawyers to fight to the bitter end at the cost of adverse publicity and a poor public image. Nevertheless, the lawyer dealing with a scientific issue will frequently assert fact that the scientist regards as settled. Lawyers and scientists should understand that their differing roles may compel differing views of reality, at least over the short run.

So much for philosophy and generalities. Let us pass now to some more important specific legal issues that toxicologists are likely to encounter in their work, first in relation to research contracts and second in relation to their regulatory responsibilities.

THE CONTRACT

The enormously increased demand for contract research and development has produced a corresponding increase in research contracts. Small and medium-sized companies generally do not have the technical or financial resources to conduct in-house development efforts such as preclinical safety studies, while even the larger companies often elect to farm out at least a part of this work. By their nature such arrangements are likely to involve highly sensitive issues, which may have economic implications far beyond the cost of the research itself. Contracts of this kind should be negotiated by a team of lawyers and scientists who have a thorough understanding of the problems to be investigated, including both the scientific issues and the potential business implications. If the research is to pursue a specific, predefined problem, such as suspected carcinogenicity, as distinguished from a general screening program, such an understanding is particularly important.

Contracts are promises that the law will enforce. The law provides remedies if a promise is breached or recognizes the performance of a promise as a duty. Contracts arise when a duty does or may come into existence, because of a promise made by one of the parties. To be legally binding as a contract, a promise must be exchanged for adequate consideration. Adequate consideration is a benefit or detriment that a party receives which reasonably and fairly induces that party to make the promise/contract.

Contracts are mainly governed by state statutory and common (judge-made) law and private law. Private law principally includes the terms of the agreement between the parties who are exchanging promises. This private law may override many of the rules otherwise established by state law. Statutory law may require some contracts be put in writing and executed with particular formalities. Otherwise, the parties may enter into a binding agreement without signing a formal written document.

In my experience, good contracting is a result of three components: legal expertise, subject matter expertise, and common sense. Assuming a modicum of common sense and a substantial understanding of the subject area of the contract, presumably contract law is the only area for which the regulatory authority (RA) professional needs knowledgeable guidance. Most of the principles of the common law of contracts are outlined in a compilation entitled *Restatement Second of The Law of Contracts* published by the American Law Institute, Philadelphia, PA. The restatements are an attempt to organize (restate) common law rules in selected broad areas (e.g. agency, contracts, conflicts of law, etc.). Restatements do not reflect statutes, which can alter common law rules and principles. Restatements are secondary authority, not law, but they are drafted by respected scholars, attorneys and jurists. They are useful as research tools and study aids.

Of greater importance is the Uniform Commercial Code (UCC), whose original articles have been adopted in nearly every US state. The UCC represents a body of statutory law that governs important categories of contracts, so it should be consulted whenever an issue arises. UCC, Article 2 regulates every phase of a transaction for the sale of goods and provides remedies for problems that may arise. It provides for implied warranties of merchantability and fitness. There is also a duty of good faith in the UCC that is applicable to all the sections.

The RA professional routinely enters into contracts, or reviews draft contract proposals, related to a wide range of goods and services necessary to develop and commercialize a regulated product. These include confidentiality agreements, and service agreements (e.g. contract manufacturing, raw material purchases, consulting agreements, clinical research organizations, and clinical investigator agreements). It is essential that the RA professional understand the essential elements of contract law (offer, acceptance, consideration, breach, remedies, etc.) as they relate to the technical aspects of their particular industry and the specific scope of contract. The effort the RA professional should invest in properly drafting or reviewing a contract is directly proportional to the criticality of the product or service to be provided. Like regulatory submissions, poorly drafted contracts can significantly affect the regulatory timetable and delay product commercialization. In particular, pay close attention when specifying the goods or services expected from the vendor. When possible, tie deliverables to ascertainable standards (GMP compliance, GCP compliance, etc.). Vague, unspecified or imprecisely defined standards often result in a legally binding agreement, but unsatisfactory deliverables.

Part of the job is to educate the lawyer about the nature of the work, including its limitations. The lawyer needs to know, for example, the extent to which test instruments and procedures are reliable, and must have a grasp of the statistical presumptions and methods so that the contract can be approached with these problems in mind. Do not assume that your lawyers are incapable of assimilating a good knowledge of the scientific issues. Their job requires them to become experts pro tem in such matters whenever they have legal relevance. Any competent lawyer should be able to understand and talk the language of toxicology and research with appropriate instruction. Many companies have sought out lawyers with technical backgrounds to make this process easier and more dependable.

Armed with this technical understanding, the lawyers can then proceed to develop a contract that is appropriate to the situation. For a low-risk, uncomplicated job they may suggest a relatively simple letter agreement with a minimum of verbiage. They might even be willing to go along with an oral understanding if the issues are very simple, but this will be rare. For a more extensive project on which substantial economic interests are riding, they will undoubtedly propose a very thorough and definitive agreement. Much of the language will be routine or 'boiler plate', the type commonly found in agreements of various kinds. Other clauses may be addressed specifically to the special problems of research contracts. What are some of these special problems?

Purpose and description of work

The basic purpose of the project should be described carefully in the contract with sufficient breadth to ensure that the researchers do not overlook something because of an inadequate understanding of the context. While some contracts may call for 'pure research' and be concerned only with the objective development of new data or information, most projects, particularly from the private sector, will have one or more very pragmatic objectives that are specific to the business purposes of the sponsor. These purposes may well affect the design and scope of the research project. For example, a pharmaceutical company may be looking for a more effective antiviral agent for use in the HIV therapeutic market. By this the company may mean that the new agent must be biologically effective for a broader range of patients, be effective in a smaller dose than the current agent, have a longer shelf life when combined with the other ingredients of the product, or have a lower incidence of side effects. Any one of these factors might justify the use of a new antiviral and could be the objective of contracted research, but it is obvious that an antiviral with more than one of these qualities would be even better. Researchers should know about these advantages so that their work can be designed for maximum usefulness and synergy with other research on the same general problem.

Of course, the sponsor may be concerned about confidentiality and may therefore want to limit the extent of the researcher's knowledge and involvement. Our producer might be aware of some emerging side-effect problem with the drugs currently on the market. Obviously, this kind of balancing is for the sponsors to decide, but they should remember that researchers working with blinders on may overlook some collateral problems and opportunities.

In addition to identifying the purpose, the contract should also identify the research methods that are to be employed. In some cases the method itself may be a subject for research, but in most situations there will be at least a general understanding of the work to be done. This should be spelled out, along with any limitations or variations from normal practice. Specific research protocols found in the literature may be adopted by reference, or the sponsor and the researcher may jointly work out a protocol of their own. There must be absolutely no ambiguity about what the researcher is called on to do.

Time frame

Much developmental research is mandated by various regulatory agencies such as the FDA, and marketing of a product may have to await the results. Thus, companies will frequently insist that time is of the essence, that the researcher must meet the stipulated timetable or be liable for damages or forfeiture of fees. Faced with such a clause, the researcher will want to be sure that he or she can in fact meet the deadlines.

Regulatory and judicial proceedings

Toxicological research data and results will often be of key importance as evidence in regulatory proceedings or in lawsuits. Hence, it is important that the work product, or at least key parts of it, be reflected in documents and records, which will be useful for this purpose. A brief overview of the applicable rules of evidence may help you understand this. These are procedural rules that are applied quite strictly in the courtroom and somewhat less strictly in administrative hearings. Basically, a document that purports to contain information that is relevant to the issue at hand cannot be admitted as evidence without first being authenticated. This means that a live witness must testify from personal knowledge that the document is genuine and that the information is in fact what it purports to be. The live witness might be the research scientist who actually produced the report or it might be a higher echelon person under whose supervision the work was done. Whoever he or she is, the live witness can expect to be the subject of intensive cross-examination, first in an attempt to show that the document is not admissible as evidence and then, if this fails, in an attempt to discredit the methods, the results, the conclusions, and indeed the competence of the researcher.

Needless to say, this can be a very stressful and unpleasant business, particularly if the document is ambiguous or incomplete or if the witness has not done the necessary homework. It can also be very time-consuming. Hence, the research contract should spell out the understanding with regard to the use of researchers as witnesses. Typically, the contract will require the research institution to supply an appropriate person or persons to testify for the purpose of authenticating and defending documents reflecting the work done. Such appearances are usually made at the expense of the interested party, including a reasonable per diem or other fee and the reimbursement of expenses. If special preparation for the appearance is anticipated, the contract should indicate whether this time is subject to special reimbursement.

Incidentally, the courts and agencies are not limited to final reports to the client in their search for relevant documentary information. It is entirely possible that research notebooks, reports of internal meetings, diaries, and even informal scratch notes may be scrutinized. CROs, like business corporations, should therefore develop carefully designed record management programs to control the creation and maintenance of formal and informal paperwork. The destruction of relevant documentation for the purpose of keeping it out of court can be a criminal offense (ask ENRON or Arthur D. Anderson). Consequently, it is important to limit the information that becomes part of the written record and to establish and observe a record retention and destruction schedule that will justify the routine weeding out of nonessential records.

For similar though not identical reasons, the contract will usually require the researcher to retain samples of tested materials, feed samples, histological specimens, and the like. These do not usually find their way into the courtroom, but may be critically important in confirming the accuracy of challenged data, rebutting allegations of misfeasance or faulty diagnosis, or accomplishing similarly constructive purposes.

As to retention period, it is almost impossible to be too conservative. The longer the better, not only to satisfy regulatory agencies and requirements but also to help establish a solid defense against future damage claims. Unfortunately for manufacturers, the statutes of limitation on claims for breach of warranty and negligence often do not begin to run until the damage or injury occurs. Thus, companies have been held liable for asserted defects in drugs taken to market decades before the damage or injury is discovered. Since both drugs and devices are an easy target in such claims, proof of adequate toxicological research can be of great defensive importance. Generally, the sponsor of a project will want samples retained for a substantial time (10 years or more) and researchers will generally share this desire in order to minimize their own potential exposure.

The long-term retention of documents and samples creates obvious storage problems. Document retention can be minimized by the disciplined use of microfilming techniques. For almost all legal purposes, a properly made and authenticated microfilm copy is equivalent to a paper original. Sample storage is a more difficult matter. The main legal problem is to be absolutely sure that each sample can be properly identified and authenticated for possible future use. Procedures for cataloging and retaining samples should be carefully worked out and scrupulously followed. This is not a mere clerical or managerial responsibility; it calls for careful and continuing management attention.

Reports

Depending on the nature and extent of the research, the contract will include provisions for reports of various kinds. Progress reports will usually be appropriate if the work is complex and extended, and a final report is routine. The parties may or may not wish such reports to include editorial matter or commentary on the results.

This raises a very difficult and potentially sensitive problem area, namely the extent to which the sponsor should be entitled to review, comment on, and edit proposed reports before they are issued. Sponsors will generally require a review of a draft report, and will often react with questions, comments, and suggestions for change. They may also want the opportunity for informal discussion of the draft report and the data and results on which it is based. There is nothing inherently wrong with this, but if the work relates to product safety and is being performed in the context of present or anticipated regulatory involvement, the parties should be extremely careful to preserve the fundamental integrity of the final report. The right to review and offer comments should never be constructed as a right to censor or suppress.

It is easy to believe and affirm that no ethical businessman, lawyer, or scientist would tolerate or encourage the suppression or distortion of research results. It is less easy to apply this faith in a specific situation, which may involve large gray areas concerning the reliability of test methods, the adequacy of samples, the significance of an occasional anomalous result, and the subjective assessment of results as a whole, not to mention the semantic nuances that can arise in the process of articulating all these issues. Because we are human, we tend to see what we want to see and to find what we want to find, if there is any room at all for doubt. The legal danger lurks in the possibility that editorial changes in a research report may be influenced, at least subliminally, by considerations of self-interest.

There are several ways to minimize this problem. First, and perhaps most obvious, the contract may simply provide that the sponsor shall have no right of prior review. Unhappily, this deprives both parties of the opportunity for legitimate synergy, and may simply be unacceptable to the sponsor. Second, the contract might provide expressly for review and comment by the sponsor but affirm the researcher's right to control the form and content of the report. This is a good approach, provided the parties do in fact observe the contract.

A third technique is to apply what might be called the 'future appearance' test to the editorial process and its end result. The test can be posed as two questions: (1) Do any of the editorial changes involve a matter that, with the benefit of future hindsight, could be viewed as having material significance in the context of any presently applicable health or safety law or regulation or reasonably foreseeable health or safety problem? and (2) If so, do the changes tend to lean toward avoiding or obscuring a potentially adverse condition?

If the answers to both questions are 'yes', the changes that produced these answers are vulnerable to future criticism and should probably be omitted or modified. Not that the first question calls for a deliberate effort to view present events from a future perspective, because that is the way our present judgments are being judged in the context of health and safety regulation.

An example may help to clarify this concept. Suppose you are engaged in some rabbit feeding studies to determine the oral toxicity of a submitted compound. At a certain point in the studies, several test animals die. Autopsy discloses gross liver damage, which is not encountered in the remaining test animals, all of which live considerably longer. You discover that an inexperienced technician may have inadvertently contaminated some of the feedstock given to the animals that died early, but you cannot prove this. There is no other obvious explanation for the early deaths. The size of the study is such that the anomalous deaths are of minimal statistical importance. Nevertheless, you decide to mention the early deaths and the liver damage in your final draft report and to include the deaths in the statistical database. Your sponsor then suggests that since the early deaths are clearly anomalous and do no affect the general conclusions of the study, it would be preferable that they be omitted from the report.

Applying the future appearances test, it seems clear that if other studies were later to confirm that liver damage is a potential side effect of the ingestion of this compound (perhaps in animals other than rabbits), it might be said, with benefit of hindsight, that your anomalous results were in fact significant. It is also clear that the requested deletion of these results would tend to minimize or discount their importance. Hence, both questions are answered affirmatively. One should reject the proposed deletion. The anomalous results should be included for what they may be worth.

If, on the other hand, the sponsor had simply requested the addition of a footnote explaining your suspicions concerning contaminated feed, this would not tend to avoid or obscure a potentially adverse conclusion. Hence, your answer to the second question would be 'no', and the requested addition would be acceptable.

Innocent mistakes and culpable tampering

A related issue, though not strictly a contract matter, is what to do when it is discovered that someone has made a significant mistake in the course of the study or has perhaps even fabricated or tampered with the results. If the work is not yet public and is not part of a submitted or approved regulatory program, it may be possible to make corrections without announcement or publicity, provided a complete record of the situation is maintained. However, if the study is part of a submitted record or an established compliance program, the best course will be to 'fess up' promptly and candidly, with an offer of full collaboration in any resultant investigation or necessary follow-up. This is embarrassing and could have serious legal consequences, but delay and/or cover-up can only make things worse.

Communications

One of the most important problems to be addressed in a research contract is communications. No matter how competent and sophisticated the work, its value will be reduced or even lost if its significance is not properly communicated to and understood by the sponsor. This is particularly true with projects whose shape and direction involve some subjective judgment or 'art' on the part of the researcher. If the implications of a judgmental decision are not made known, the sponsor may be deprived of important information for the evaluation and utilization of the results.

Therefore, the contract should specify the method or methods of communication, the timing (if there are to be interim reports), the circumstances, if any, in which a special report may be appropriate, and the channels through which communications are to be made. Each project will have its own specific needs, but generally speaking, the broader or more loosely defined the methods and objectives, the greater the need for ongoing close communication between the parties.

Since scientific issues and judgments will invariably be involved, the sponsor should designate specific scientific personnel in its organization as the initial recipients of reports. It is not uncommon to designate a manager for each project, with responsibility to receive all reports, communicate as appropriate with the researcher, and distribute the reports within the organization.

The communication of new information can have important legal implications for both parties. The researcher will have a duty to report any significant adverse results or effects as promptly as possible, while actual knowledge of such things may trigger a reporting responsibility on the part of the sponsor, either under the FDA or under some other regulatory bodies' requirements on a common-law duty. For this reason it is critically important to maintain a good record of all communications on matters of potential significance. In addition to copies of written reports, it may be appropriate to maintain a log of telephone or other oral communications and a record of any meetings between the parties. The phone log can simply be a record of calls made, giving date, time, and names of the communicants. If the project is likely to produce sensitive interim information, it may be wise to go further and include a brief synopsis of the conversation. The same options apply to meeting records.

This raises a difficult policy question for both parties. If they elect to keep separate records, there is always the chance that the two records may be inconsistent in some important respect. This could produce embarrassment in the future. On the other hand, if the parties decide to maintain a single record of their communications or to compare notes, the editorial dangers discussed earlier will obviously be raised.

Whatever the record-keeping protocol, it is a good idea to be consistent when following the agreed procedure. Variations from a customary pattern are favorite clues for hostile lawyers to find evidence of malfeasance, nonfeasance, or cover-up. Nothing is more intriguing and suspicious than a hole in a file at some critically important time.

The problem of communication also embraces some very difficult judgmental questions for the researcher whose work uncovers some new and perhaps significant information. What constitutes a reportable event, and when should it be reported? The basic standard is one of reasonableness and good faith. For the purpose, reasonableness will be judged in relation to your scientific expertise and sophistication – the 'reasonable scientist' test. If it would be reasonable for a competent scientist to believe that the development is materially significant in relation to the regulatory purpose or some other legal issue, it should be reported to the sponsor, even though you yourself might not share this belief. If, in good faith, that scientist does not believe that the development is significant in this sense, it need not be reported immediately, although it may become a part of some later routine report.

Proprietary rights

If the research is of such nature that original methods, techniques, or equipment may have to be developed, the contract should deal with the problem of ownership and right of use. Generally, parties who pay for the research will want to own any resultant inventions, although they may be willing to give shop rights to the researcher for applications that are not adverse to their particular interests. A research company may be reluctant to surrender the right to further use of its own inventions. Obviously these problems should be addressed in the contract. The final result will depend on the bargaining. Even with a well-drawn contract, difficult problems can sometimes arise in the problem area.

Confidentiality

Every research contract should include a clause dealing with the use and disclosure of proprietary information. The first, often difficult step is to define what is meant by proprietary information. Although many judicial decisions attempt to define this term, the peculiar nature of research will often justify a carefully drafted contractual definition based on the specific situation. The clause should cover both information supplied to the researchers by the sponsoring party and information developed by the researchers in the course of their work. The party supplying data will want the broadest possible definition, usually one that attempts to cover all submitted information regardless of whether it is actually proprietary or a trade secret. Researchers, on the other hand, should be careful not to accept an excessively broad clause that might seriously hamper their legal or ethical responsibilities.

A very common traditional approach is to restrict the use and disclosure of all submitted information except in three specific categories: (1) information known to the disclosee prior to disclosure, (2) information properly available to the disclosee from another source and without restriction, and (3) information in the public domain.

Despite its popularity, this approach can pose problems for parties involved in research because the traditional language does not adequately protect a party's rights with respect to the future fruits of ongoing or incipient projects. For example, if a research organization has begun a line of inquiry that may lead to valuable new information or methodology, the receipt of related data from another party under conditions that restrict its use may becloud the freedom of researchers to pursue their pre-existing inquiry along its logical path. For this reason, each party to a proposed research agreement should carefully review his or her then-current activities to determine whether the confidential receipt of information would be likely to cause any problems with other projects. If a problem is foreseen, the lawyer may be able to draft contract language to reduce or avoid the difficulty. The confidentiality clause should also cover such questions as mandatory disclosure to government agencies, limitations on the persons within the contracting organizations who will be allowed access (frequently limited to those who have a 'need to know'), and limitations on publication rights, if any. If there are to be subcontracts, the confidentiality clause should be extended to cover the subcontractors.

In conclusion, it should be clear that there is almost no such thing as a routine research contract and that an adequate contract demands close cooperation and mutual understanding between the lawyers and the scientists involved. The contract may end up looking simple and commonplace, but its underlying homework should always be thorough.

Ethical and legal problems of regulatory disclosure

It should be obvious by now that many scientists involved in research may need help in understanding the legal aspects of their position. There is nothing wrong with using the company's law department or legal counsel as a first recourse, but bear in mind that they represent the employer, not the individual researcher. These remain, ultimately, personal ethical issues to resolve.

Monitoring Ongoing Studies and Work

Once work is initiated at a vendor, steps must be taken to ensure the progress, quality, and conformance with regulatory requirements of the work performed. This is achieved by an active program of monitoring of ongoing work. Such monitoring can be performed either by client employees or by contract monitors, but those conducting such auditors must have suitable skills, experience and knowledge to serve this purpose successfully. The earliest text on the subject that I am aware of (Gralla, 1981) is still valuable though now significantly dated.

Such a monitoring program should be planned and scheduled in advance, and as such must be considered an integral part of the project. While for purposes of example the case of a toxicology study operating under Good Laboratory Practices (GLPs) is considered, the general principles are operative for GMP and GCP situations, and references are provided for these.

IN-PROGRESS MONITORING

As mentioned before, 'Compliance Inspection Manuals' which are used by inspectors in their agency laboratory inspection programs are available from the FDA (FDA, 1984). The manuals offer a systematic and thorough means of reviewing elements of GLP compliance and can serve as guides regarding standardized aspects of laboratories and studies. The reader is also referred to the audit check list provided in Appendix I. The results of prior regulatory inspections may also be accessed on line (FDA, 2002).

Having carefully evaluated the laboratory before contracting the study, the focus of in-progress monitoring changes from general to specific. Whereas initially the animal feed room was inspected for cleanliness, good housekeeping, and a rodent-free environment, now the feed should be inspected to see if it is segregated and logged out at suitable times and in amounts proportional to specific study needs.

Likewise, much of the other in-progress monitoring will focus on data which have already been gathered. In performing this review, notes should be made and a list of items prepared for discussion with facility and study management at an exit conference. In-progress monitoring should also include review of vivarium conditions (temperature, humidity) and animal husbandry records. Although not the most fascinating data to review, the conditions under which the animals are housed can seriously influence the study's outcome, both from a biological point of view as well as relative to the study's acceptability by regulatory agencies.

All data pertaining to clinical observations, blood and clinical chemistry analyses, weights, and feed consumption statistics should be reviewed. Not all of these may apply and some studies will have more complex in-life observations than described here.

The laboratory's QA inspection reports should be reviewed at this time. These reports should demonstrate that QA inspections are being carried out according to QA standard operating procedures (SOPs). The content of the reports should be reviewed as a means of ensuring adherence to the study protocol and the laboratory's SOPs.

The purpose of an in-progress monitoring visit is to review all the data collected since the last visit in order to ascertain that the study is progressing smoothly and without major problems. The data reviewed should be generally consistent with the sponsor's understanding of study progress derived from previous inspections or reports from the laboratory. If the study appears to be changing in unsuspected ways, the sponsor and the study director should discuss the possibility of alteration of the study design: adding more or different observations, adjusting doses or dosing schedules, inserting an unplanned interim sacrifice. The study protocol is designed to accommodate all reasonably foreseeable events in the study. However, some events may occur which were unexpected, particularly in a complex study. The monitoring visit allows the opportunity for the sponsor and study director to adapt the study design, if necessary.

If the study design has been changed since the sponsor's last visit, protocol amendments which clearly state the change, its scope, and the reason for the change should be found in the study documentation. If the amendment was authorized by the sponsor during a previous communication, this should be referred to.

The facility's SOPs should again be checked to ensure that relevant procedures are being followed (from cage washing to histological preparation).

Most procedures generate some kind of documentation which should be reviewed.

When all available documentation has been reviewed, the sponsor will have a list of items for discussion with study management. Sponsor and study director, together with other pertinent laboratory staff (pathologist, animal care supervisor, quality assurance staff) should meet to resolve these issues.

Generally, the questions can be resolved fairly easily. Sometimes things go wrong which are beyond the control of facility management, such as temperature or humidity excursions in the animal room. If not numerous, extreme, or cyclical, such excursions are probably of little importance. However, if patterns of consistent difficulties are detected, facility management should be required to improve its control over environmental conditions. This may involve moving the study to a different room for completion or providing the facility maintenance staff with additional instruction and training. Whatever the cause, the desired effect is correction of excessive environmental variation.

Since the laboratory was selected on the basis of a thorough preplacement evaluation, now is the time to ask laboratory management to bring its expertise to bear on whatever problems have arisen in the study.

What if major problems arise which warrant aborting the study and restarting it? A frank discussion with study management (and your own management!) should be the starting point. If the sponsor's judgment to abort comes as the result of in-progress monitoring without any previous idea that such serious deficiencies existed, the sponsor's and the study director's views are apparently far apart. If, on the other hand, the sponsor's inspection is the result of the laboratory's report of problems, then the decision to restart the study may be easily and jointly reached.

The contract confers rights and responsibilities on both parties, and should therefore be consulted if study abortion and restart is contemplated. If the contract clearly permits the sponsor to judge at what point a major problem or a series of minor problems constitutes grounds for aborting the study, the decision to do so should be made expeditiously. Having learned from the experience, sponsor and study director should proceed to restart the study with as little delay as possible.

THE STUDY REPORT

Most sponsors will want interim reports for major long-term studies. Since the interim reports will form the basis for the final report, they should be read carefully and critically. If misinformation, confidential business information, or poor interpretations of data are presented in the interim reports, they should be corrected at once. Interim reports may also be sought by regulators, so they should be held to the same exacting standards of thoroughness and accuracy as the final report.

The final report should be presented to the sponsor in draft form. Several years ago, this was a contested notion, with many contract laboratories objecting to draft reports. However, the current practice is for contract laboratories to submit drafts for review by sponsors.

The study report should contain all essential elements, generally those covered in GLP regulations. Additional data may be included, for example, information about the test material, interpretative statements by sponsor scientists, references to other studies of the test material, or a host of other information. The sponsor should make such inclusions after receipt of the final report from the testing laboratory. For example, if previous study data are relevant, they might usefully be included in a discussion section.

Much report information required by GLPs deals with methodological details which should have been carefully described in the protocol. Appending the protocol to the study report can serve to fulfill these requirements. This saves time and retains the study plan as a historical document. If the protocol was not strictly followed or if it required extensive alterations, a new description of methodology may be preferable.

The final study report should contain signatures of all required parties: study director, QA inspector, pathologist, statistician, clinical chemist, and any other scientists who contributed significantly to the work. It is also a good idea to list the study personnel. Such personnel can change frequently, and personnel lists may not be available if there is a need to identify study staff at some time in the future.

The study report should take no more than two drafts in order for sponsor and contract laboratory to agree on a final version. If the sponsor feels that additional drafts are needed, this should be resolved quickly with the contract laboratory. Frequently there is a reluctance to rewrite reports many times, and the zeal with which the perfect report is pursued will diminish with time. A qualified scientist is entitled to disagree with conclusions reached by another in an addendum to the report, although agreeing on the conclusions drawn from the study at the outset is a less awkward means of presenting conclusions in the report. Nevertheless it is not uncommon for a sponsor's final report to include statements of opinion differing from those offered by the contract laboratory.

SUBCONTRACTED SERVICES

The contract laboratory may not have available all the services needed to complete the study. For example, some laboratories use contract pathology services. Archiving of raw data, specimens, samples, and interim and final reports may be done at a commercial archiving operation rather than at the laboratory. Prior to contracting, decisions need to be made concerning services which the laboratory itself will not provide. In the case where pathology is subcontracted, the sponsor should be able to specify a pathology laboratory other than the one the contract laboratory usually uses. Likewise, if the contractor does not have its own archive space, the samples could be retained by the sponsor, rather than having them sent to a commercial archivist or warehouse. These issues should be anticipated and addressed in the contract. If circumstances require a change in the planned provider of these services, sponsor and contract laboratory should keep each other informed.

ONGOING CONTRACTS

Having successfully completed a contracted study, if the sponsor anticipates a continuing need, developing an ongoing contract with this laboratory for future work should be considered. Establishing a continuing relationship with one or several laboratories enables the sponsor to familiarize the laboratory thoroughly with the sponsor's study methods as well as with any idiosyncrasies of reporting or data gathering. In addition, economies can usually be effected on the basis of volume and/or regular scheduling. Also, establishing an ongoing relationship with a contract laboratory may improve the turnaround time of 'rush' studies, since the laboratory might be able to accommodate such a request more easily for an established than for a one-time customer.

Many sponsors have found it useful to establish such ongoing testing contracts with several laboratories simultaneously. Some advantages of this approach are: expanding the possibilities of squeezing in a 'rush' study, extending the standardization of test methodology from the sponsor's perspective, and increasing the objectivity of the overall testing program by bringing several observation and judgment capabilities to bear on similar methods and data sets.

A fourth advantage is that failures of individual contract laboratories will not leave a sponsor's testing program grounded so that the process of finding a suitable laboratory must be begun again.

Some specialties are well practiced in only a handful of laboratories. In these cases, the objective must be to get a good study done each time. More and closer overseeing may be required in such cases than if several laboratories are adept and ready to do the required testing.

REFERENCES

FDA (1984). *Compliance Program Guidance Manual*, Chapter 48, Human drugs and biologics: Bioresearch monitoring. FDA, Washington, DC.

FDA (2002). List of Inspected Nonclinical Laboratories Since FY '90, http://www.fda.gov/org/.compliance ref/bimo/GLP/default.htm

GRALLA, E.J. (1981). *Scientific Considerations in Monitoring and Evaluating Scientific Work*. Hemisphere Publishing, New York.

Common Problems and their Solutions

Despite the best efforts and intentions of all involved, there will always be an incidence of problems even in successful subcontracting (many of these problems are also present when work is performed using internal resources, but such are not the subject of this volume). What can be done is to be aware of such problems and to be prepared to solve them if they arise. Preferably the initial step to a solution is knowledge of how others have previously solved similar problems.

In each of the cases that follow a first step might well be to avoid the situations in the first place. So for each of the common problems that are considered, an example of how some arose is provided.

CHANGES IN KEY PERSONNEL

Part of the initial selection process for a contractor is based on the experience and qualifications of their staff. Unfortunately, such assumptions may not hold true in at least two cases.

In the first case, key personnel may leave the organization through changing jobs, disability, or death. In the second situation, a key individual (such as a study director in a toxicology study) may prove to look better on paper than in reality and not be up to the job. In either of these cases, a central figure involved in the completion of desired work is no longer present or involved.

Avoiding the occurrence of this problem is difficult, other than assuring the on the job (as opposed to on paper) competence of key individuals to the fullest extent possible. The other causes are generally not subject to *a priori* prediction or avoidance.

When faced with this situation, there are three potential solutions. The first is to have the vendor reassign another suitable individual to fill the vacancy – should such a person be available. Unfortunately, it is uncommon that this is possible owing to limited redundancy within vendor (or nowadays, any) organizations.

The second approach is to hire (or, rather, have the vendor organization hire) a suitable person for the completion of the task. The vendor may know such individuals, or a search of the appropriate website (e.g. www.toxconsultants.com for a toxicologist or www.chemconsultants.com for a chemist) may provide candidates. This is the more common approach, with the effective subcontract being limited to the period of need. The third approach (generally viable if a project has not yet actually been initiated) is to delay the start or completion of a project until a full time replacement is hired.

CLIENT SIGNING PROTOCOLS

When work is contracted out there is a tendency in many organizations to maintain (and even diffuse) control and authority even though technical skills are not present. This is most commonly experienced by sponsors as well as contracted experts (consultants/monitors) being signatories for protocols, amendments, and other documents. This leads to (at best) a lack of clarity in lines of authority and responsibility for decisions, and perhaps much worse. In such a situation, most contractors will take no action until there is consensus or clarity, which in nonclinical and clinical studies often becomes an (unintended) decision itself.

The means of avoiding this problem are clear, having only a single technical signatory from the sponsor regardless of whether said individual is internal to the sponsor or a consultant at project initiation. The worst case, by the way, is rare in the pharmaceutical industry but common in other industries (such as chemicals) – a committee in charge. Enough said. If, however, this problem cannot be avoided then ensuring open and continuous communications is essential.

TIME SLIPPAGE

The most valuable asset in the development of new products in the industries that we are concerned with is not money, but rather time. This leads to most activities being precisely scheduled (either to ensure the quickest time to overall project completion or the optimal use of resources such as money). While (as was made clear earlier) a clean set of expectations on completion must be part of the contracting process, nature and the course of human events may preclude on-time completion. Any extra time available between the initiation of an activity and its scheduled or required completion (delivery of a report or drug substance or for mutated dosage form) constitutes 'float' in the terminology of project management, and must be carefully preserved. Small delays which on their own seem trivial all too often accumulate to produce a painful protraction in completion. A frequent admonition to clients and contractors is 'don't eat my float and I won't eat yours'.

Delays can arise from a vast number of causes, but usually these translate to a shortage of a resource (equipment, materials, test animals, manpower, or an essential skill set such as expertise with using a specific instrument or the performance of a necropsy on test animals). When such are identified their impact is commonly underestimated. The key to avoiding or minimizing the impact of these is to ensure that causative factors and events are identified as soon as they occur, and that corrective actions are initiated as rapidly as possible. A second step is to allow some level of redundancy of resources to be included in plans. Extra starting material for synthesis or a few extra animals on hand over the minimal requirements are cheap insurance for on-time completion of the projects in question.

If such events still come to pass, then the best means of minimizing their impact is to provide a supplement or replacement for the limiting (critical path) source of the completion of the entire project (i.e. drug or device approval).

REGULATORY NONCOMPLIANCE

The industries that we are concerned with here are heavily regulated in virtually all aspects. Small occurrences of noncompliance with such regulation (such as not taking samples of dosing solutions for analysis or not following quality assurance procedures) can invalidate entire studies, leading at best to a need for repetition of the same or additional work (and time).

All such regulated activities now must have some form of quality system (QS) in place. Regulatory noncompliance in such situations can occur only if the QS was incomplete (overlooked in the initial system set up) or failed. Avoiding such occurrences is best achieved in the pre-award phase of contract work. Initially, ensure that necessary systems are in place (evidenced by SOPs, validation reports, and quality assurance unit (and such) operatives) and effective for the critical points/activities involved in the work to be performed. Subsequent to this there should be a program of monitoring ongoing works. Consider having a full systems (GLP/GMP/GCP) audit performed on any facility which is either doing a large, critical project or providing a number of separate projects.

If a noncompliance issue is identified, the solution is to document both the problem and corrective action in a timely manner.

QUALITY CONTROL/ASSURANCE FAILURES

Again there are several aspects of this topic. The first is if quality assurance and control procedures are not followed. An example is when plasma samples from a group of volunteers or subjects are analyzed and lead to erroneously high or low reported levels of the agent of interest. The second is when the understanding of regulatory quality assurance or study design requirements on the part of contractor personnel are different from those of the sponsor. Such differences of opinion can be legitimate, but the impact on cost, quality, and timing are potentially enormous.

This issue has some degree of overlap with regulatory noncompliance. Here I wish to focus on aspects not covered under that other topic: (1) that there is a significant disagreement between the contractor's quality assurance and the client's professional opinion (experience) or (2) that a QC/QA failure caused actions to be taken which cannot be solved simply by documenting the event and taking action afterwards.

The first of these can take several forms: that a quality problem has or has not occurred; or in some contract organizations, what is or is not presented in a report. For these, both the client and vendor management must be involved to arrive at a mutually acceptable solution.

The second case is harder. If an erroneous finding has caused an irreversible action to be taken (such as shutting down a clinical trial or making a regulatory filing which was incorrect), fixing the matter has two separate aspects. First, all involved must be notified in writing of the error. Second, a legal issue of restitution of damages will need to be resolved between the client and vendor.

INAPPROPRIATE TECHNOLOGY

This may be due to decisions by the sponsor or the contractor (or both). The former may have an existing analytical method which served them well during earlier work on a project (such as an RIA method for measuring drug levels instead of a more sensitive LC/MS method) and do not want to spend the money or delay progress on work while a better method is developed.

Contractors, on the other hand, usually play to their strength. If they have certain equipment and methods on hand, such are likely to constitute the recommended means of addressing a problem. An example here might be using a mass balance approach with a limited number of organs to evaluate the distribution of a drug and its metabolites throughout the body, as opposed to using whole-body autoradiography.

It behooves both the client and vendor to ensure that technologies involved in project conduct are either according to the current industry norm or that there is a well documented reason otherwise.

If it is found that the methodology employed does not meet current regulatory expectations (despite the rationale behind its use being good), then a bridging study establishing that the results are comparable with those from the desired method (or animal species) is advisable.

FACILITY SHUTDOWN

Sometimes a facility will cease operations while work on a study or project is still ongoing. Causes of such situations in the past have included financial failure, death of essential personnel, and an acquisition of the facility by new management. Due diligence before contract award is the best means to avoid this problem. Make sure the financial stability of a laboratory and other factors cited here are evaluated before an award.

Such an occurrence, if detected in a timely manner, can be addressed in one of two ways. Either the means may be acquired or negotiated (in the case of an acquisition) to resume operations and continue them until the contracted task is completed, or the work can be moved to another facility for completion. The past has seen entire colonies of laboratory animals relocated in just such circumstances.

ACTS OF NATURE

Natural disasters do happen. Floods, hurricanes (wiping out animal colonies), fires and earthquakes are all possibilities that can disrupt or totally discontinue conduct of development activities. The occurrence of these cannot be either predicted or avoided but the ability of a facility to withstand such occurrences and continue operations can and must be evaluated as a part of pre-award considerations.

CROs MAY STRETCH THE TRUTH

While in my experience this has become much less of a problem than it once was, it still occurs that contractors may claim that they have capabilities that they don't, or can meet timelines which have more of a spiritual than managerial basis. Avoidance of this problem is best pursued by careful review of past performance. While asking for and checking with provided reference clients is a useful step, a sponsor should also use their professional contacts to seek out and query a broader range of prior clients.

The degree of the problem dictates the appropriate response. If the contractor has been over-optimistic about their ability to provide timely results, this can be addressed as previously discussed under time slippage. But if an actual untruth is detected, the problem is much more serious. Impact and corrective actions after such a breach of faith must be carefully considered.

SILENT SUBCONTRACTORS

Just as sponsors subcontract, so do contractors. Very common cases for toxicology labs, for example, include pathology, bioanalytical and analytical chemistry, and statistical analysis. It may not be made clear to the client that such is the case before a project is initiated. It is thus essential that documents such as protocols clearly disclose any subcontractors and their specific responsibilities, as well as providing sufficient contract information to allow an independent sponsor contract and follow-up.

ALLIANCES

Again, just as with client organizations, there may exist informal or formal arrangements between contractors which can influence, complicate, or impede progress on a project. Examples include: (1) a data entry analysis CRO which will not provide support to phase I studies initiated at other than their 'partner' clinical facility once work has been done at that facility and (2) a GMP synthesis facility which has an arrangement with specific formulation and CTM manufacturing organizations.

Such arrangements do not inherently cause any harm, but should be disclosed at the beginning and in no way bind the sponsor to use (or even consider) the contractor's related organizations. Any 'alliance' organizations must be evaluated on their own independent merits.

Sponsors must insist on full and timely disclosure of any such arrangements and evaluate any resulting impact.

TOO MANY EGGS IN A BASKET

While there are both good reasons and a natural tendency to 'reward' a vendor that performs well with additional works, it is always a sound practice to have more than a single contractor available to conduct a particular type of work (if at all possible). There are several reasons for this.

Even the best of contract service providers have limits on how much work they can do, and also will be subject to circumstances beyond their control from time to time.

These occurrences can easily lead to: (1) having to accept delays or compromises in study or task performance or (2) in some cases finding that you are (in effect) competing against yourself for resources on different projects.

The essential solution to this problem is to be aware of viable alternative providers, and if possible to have the necessary preparation work (site visits, confidentiality agreements and such) in place in advance. It is even well advised to split workloads between two separate vendors – while the cost of operations may be modestly increased in the short run, such an arrangement can be used to manage costs better (and even decrease them) in the long run.

Toxicology Labs

Lab	Location	Phone #	Website	Additional Services	Rat	Rabbits	Dog	Carcinogenicity	DART	Inhalation	Primate	Pig	IV Infusion	Genotoxic	Devices	Metabolism	Analytical	Special Studies
ABC Labs	Missouri, IA; N. Ireland, UK	(573) 474-8579; +44 (0) 2870 320639	www.abclabs.com	Bioanalysis, methods development	X											X	X	
Applied Preclinical Services	Oxford, NJ	(908) 637-4427	NO															
Austrian Research Center	Seibersdorf, Austria	+43(0) 50550-0	www.arcs.ac.at		X		X		X			X				X		SP
BAS	West Lafayette, IN	(800) 845-4246	www.bioanalytical.com	Yes	X	X	X	X		X	X	X	X	X		X	X	
Battelle	Columbus, OH	(800) 201-2011	www.battelle.org	Yes	X	X	X	X		X	X	X	X	X		X	X	
BEC Labs	Richland, WA; Toledo, OH	(419) 693-5307; (888) BEC-LABS	www.beclabs.com	Yes	X		X	X		X					X			
Bio-Life	Neillsville, WI	(715) 743-3171	NO	Yes														
BioReliance	Rockville, MD	(800) 738-1000	www.bioreliance.com	*Full range: genotoxicity, Transgenic mouse CA models, MPI p53	X	X							X	X	X		X	WL
Biotechnics	Hillsborough, NC	(919) 245-3114	www.biotechnics-inc.com	Yes	X	X	X							X				
BRI	Vancouver, BC	(604) 432-9237	www.bripharm.com	Yes, pharmaceutical, development, +	X	X	X							X		X	X	
BRT	Raleigh, NC	(919) 851-4499	www.futurecity.com/ westwood/saks/135/brt/ location.html	*Specialty immunotox	X	X									X			
BTC	Irvine, CA	(949) 660-3185	www.biologicaltestcenter.com	Yes, pediatrics, +	X	X	X	X		X	X					X	X	
Calvert	Olyphant, PA	(570) 586-2411	www.calvertlabs.com	Yes	X	X	X	X			X		X	X	X	X	X	
Celsis	St. Louis, MO	(314) 487-6776	www.celsislabs.com	Yes, stability, methods	X						X			X	X	X	X	SP

Company	Location	Phone	Website	Services / Notes	Marks
Central Toxicology Labs. (Sygenta)	Alderley Park, Macclesfield SK10 4TJ, UK	+44 16255 15852 (p) +44 16255 17314 (f)	www.syngenta.com	Yes	X X X X X X X X SP
Cerep	Redmond, WA	(425) 895-8666	www.cerep.com	Chemistry, in vitro HERG, ion channels	SP
Chantest	Cleveland, OH	(216) 332-1665 (p) (216) 332-1706 (f)	www.chantest.com		
Charles River	Worchester, MA	(978) 658-6000	www.criver.com	Tumor models, implant studies	X X X X X X SP
	Redfield, AR			*Primates, immunotox	X X X X X X X
	Sparks, NV	(877) 274-8371			X X X X X
				*Phototoxicity	X
Cirion	Horsham, PA Spencerville, OH Canada	(419) 647-4196 (450) 688-6445	www.cirion.ca	Yes, clinical	X X X X X X
CIT - Centre Internat. De Toxicologie	France	+33 2 32 292626 (p) +33 2 32 678705 (f)	www.citox.com		X X X X X X X X X SP
Commonwealth Biotechnologies Inc.	Richmond, VA	(804) 648-3820	www.cbi-biotech.com	Genomics	X
Comparative Biosciences	Mountain View, CA	(650) 404-0941 (p) (650) 404-0944 (f)	www.compbio.com	*Special discovery, models	X X X X X
Covance	Vienna, VA Madison, WI Harrogate, U.K. Muenster, Germany	(888) COVANCE (888) 541-LABS	www.covance.com	Clinical, consulting	X X X X X X X X SP; X X SP
CPTC	Fairfield, NJ	(973) 808-7111	www.cptclabs.com	Yes, clinical +	X X
Dermtech	San Diego, CA	(800) 808-2774	www.dermtechintl.com		X X X
Enviro-Bio-Tech-Ltd.	Bernville, PA	(610) 488-7664	NO	Yes, consulting (chicken, cattle) (food animals)	X X WL
Exygen	State College, PA	(800) 281-3219 (p) (800) 272-1019 (f)	www.exygen.com	Methods, development	X X X X
Fraunhofer ITA	Nikolai-Fuchs-Str., D-30625, Hannover, Germany	+49 511 5353 0 (p) +49 511 5353 155(f)	www.ita.fhg.de		X X X X X X X
Gwathmey	Cambridge, MA	(617) 491-0022 (p) (617) 492-5545 (f)	www.gwathmey.com	Consulting, biology	X X X

Lab	Location	Phone #	Website	Additional Services	Rat	Rabbits	Dog	Carcinogenicity	DART	Inhalation	Primate	Pig	IV Infusion	Genotoxic	Devices	Metabolism	Analytical	Special Studies
Huntingdon	East Millstone, NJ	(732) 873-2550	www.huntingdon.com	Discovery support	X	X	X	X	X	X	X	X	X			X	X	
	Cambridgeshire, UK	+44 (0) 1480 892000			X	X	X	X	X	X	X	X		X		X	X	SP
IITRI	Chicago, IL	(312) 567-4000	www.iitri.com	Yes	X			X	X	X						X		
ILS	McLean, VA	(703) 918-4480																
	RTP, NC	(919) 544-5857	www.ils-limited.co.uk	Data analysis, ecotoxicology	X		X	X	X		X	X	X	X		X	X	SP
Inveresk	Tranent, Scotland	+44 (0) 1875 614555	www.inveresk.com	Clinical	X	X	X	X	X	X	X	X	X	X		X	X	SP
	Montreal, QU	(514) 630-8200			X	X	X	X	X	X	X	X	X			X	X	SP
Irvine Analytical Labs, Inc.	Irvine, CA	(877) 445-6554	www.ialab.com	Yes					X	X						X	X	
ITR	Montreal, OU	(514) 457-7400	www.itrlab.com	Affiliated labs	X	X	X	X	X	X	X	X	X	X		X	X	SP
ITRI	Albuquerque, NM	(408) 428-9988	www.itri.com	Yes	X	X	X	X	X	X						X	X	
LABS	Laval, Canada	(450) 973-2240	www.preclin.com	Yes	X	X	X	X	X		X	X	X	X		X		
Liberty Research	Waverly, NY	(607) 565-8131 (p)	NO	Cats, ferrets	X	X	X											
		(607) 565-7420 (f)																
Lovelace	Albuquerque, NM	(505) 348-9456	www.lrri.org	Clinical						X								
MB Research	Spinnerstown, PA	(215) 536-4110	www.mbresearch.com	In vitro and alternative models	X									X				
MDS Pharma Services	Lincoln, NE	(425) 487-8277	www.mdsps.com	Clinical, receptor screening	X			X						X	X	X	X	
	L'Arbresle, France																	
	Geneva, Switzerland																	
Medtox s.r.l.	via Trinacria 34, I-92125 Catiania, Italy	+39 95 223027 (p)	NO		X			X						X	X	X	X	SP
		+39 95 222919 (f)			X			X						X	X	X	X	SP

Name	Location	Phone	Website	Services
Micro Test	Agawam, MA	(800) 631-1680	www.microtestlabs.com	Yes
MPI	Mattawan, MI	(269) 668-3336	www.mpi.com	Yes
MSI	Minato-ku, Tokyo, Japan	+81 3 3454 7571	www.ankaken.co.jp	Yes
MWRI	Kansas City, MO	(816) 753-7600	www.mriresearch.org	Yes
NAMSA	Toledo, OH / Irvine, CA / Kennesaw, GA	(419) 666-9455 / (949) 951-3110 / (770) 427-3101	www.namsa.com	Yes
Nelson Labs	Salt Lake City, UT	(800) 826-2088	www.nelsonlabs.com	Yes
Northern Biomedical Research	Muskegon, MI	(231) 759-2333		Yes, surgery, large animals
Northview	Northbrook, IL / Hercules, CA / Spartan, SC	(847) 564-8181 / (510) 694-9000 / (864) 574-7728	www.northviewlabs.com	Yes
NOTOX	s'Hertogenbosch, the Netherlands	+31 73 640 67 00 (p) / +31 73 640 67 99 (f)	www.notox.nl	Yes, birds, +
Nucro-Technics	Ontario, Canada	(416) 438-6727 (p) / (416) 438-3463 (f)	www.nucro-technics.com	Microbiology
PPI	Doylestown, PA	(215) 348-3868	www.ppicro.com	Yes, chemical, in vivo
Product Safety Labs	Dayton, NJ	(732) 438-5100 (732) 254-9200	www.productsafetylabs.com	Environmental
Quest	Newark, Delaware	(302) 369-5601	www.questpharm.com	Yes
Quintiles	Ledbury, UK & US	+44 (0) 131 451 2560 / (877) 988-2100	www.quintiles.com	Yes, clinical, development +
Rallis Research Center	Bangalore, India		www.rallis.co.in	
RCC Ltd.	Zelgliweg 1, CH-4452 Itegen, Switzerland	(410) 385-1666 (US sales office) / +41 61 975 1111 (p)	www.rcc.ch	Consulting, regulatory
Ricerca	Concord, OH	(888) 763-4797	www.ricerca.com	*Synthesis, product development
RTC S.p.A.	via Tito Speri 12, I-40 Pomezia, (Rom), Italy	+39 06 910 951 (p) / +39 06 910 5737 (f)	www.rtc.it	Yes, consulting, regulatory

Lab	Location	Phone #	Website	Additional Services	Rat	Rabbits	Dog	Carcinogenicity	DART	Inhalation	Primate	Pig	IV Infusion	Genotoxic	Devices	Metabolism	Analytical	Special Studies
RTI	RTP, NC	(919) 541-6000	www.rti.org	Yes	X	X	X	X	X	X			X	X	X	X	X	
SafePharm	Derby, UK	+44 (0) 1332 792896	www.safepharm.com	Yes, (fish+)	X	X	X	X	X	X			X	X	X	X	X	
SCANTOX	Hestehavevej 36a, DK-4623, Lille Skensved, Denmark	+45 56 82 11 00 (p) +45 56 82 12 02 (f)	www.scantox.com		X	X	X	X	X	X		X	X	X	X	X	X	SP
Sequani Limited	Bromyard Road, Herefordshire, HR8 1LH, Ledbury, UK	+44 1531 634121 (p) +44 1531 634753 (f)	www.sequani.com		X	X	X	X	X			X	X	X	X			
SGS	Fairfield, NJ	(800) 777-8378	www.ustesting.sgsna.com	Yes, combustion, fish, industrial, consumer products		X								X	X		X	SP, WL
Sitek	Rockville, MD	(301) 926-4900	www.siteklabs.com	Yes	X	X	X	X	X					X	X	X	X	
Skeletech	Bothell, WA	(425) 424-2663	www.skeletech.com	*Bone, CNS	X	X	X	X	X		X	X	X	X	X	X		
SNBL	Kagoshima, Japan	+81 (0) 99-294-2600 +81 (0) 99-294-3196 (f)	www.snbl.com	Yes, clinical, ferrets +	X	X	X	X	X	X	X	X	X	X				SP
SNBL USA Ltd.	6605 Merrill Creek Parkway, Everett, WA 98203	(425) 407 0121 (p) (425) 407 8601 (f)	http://www.snblusa.com/	Formulation, ferrets	X	X	X	X	X	X	X	X	X	X			X	SP
Southern RI	Birmingham, AL	(888) 322-1166	www.southernreaserch.org	Yes, formulation, development, tumor models	X	X	X	X	X	X	X	X	X	X	X	X	X	SP
SP1-bio	France	+33 (0) 169 53 14 00	www.spibio.com	Clinical	X											X	X	
Spring Valley Lab.	Woodbine, MD	(800) 864-1839	www.springvalleylabs.com	Yes	X	X								X		X	X	

Company	Location	Phone	Website	Additional services	Special
SRI	Palo Alto, CA	(650) 859-3000	www.sri.com	Yes, ocular	
Stillmeadow Inc.	Sugarland, TX	(281) 240-8828	www.stillmeadow.com		
STS duo Tek	Rush, NY / Henrietta, NY	(716) 321-1130 / (800) 836-4850	www.stsduotek.com		
TherImmune	Gaithersburg, MD	(301) 330-3733	www.therimmune.com	Yes	SP
TNO Pharma	Utrechtseweg 48, NL-3700AJ Zeist, 3704 HE, the Netherlands	+31 30 694 4806 (p) / +31 30 694 4845 (f)	www.voeding.tno.nl	Yes, packaging, food & nutrition, clinical	SP, WL
TOXIKON Corp.	15 Wiggins Ave. Bedford, MA 01730	(781) 275 3330 (p) / (781) 271-1136 (f)	www.toxikon.com	Yes	WL
UIC Tox Research Lab	Chicago, IL	(312) 996-2123	www.uic.edu/labs/tox	Yes	
Viromed	Minneapolis, MN	(800) 582-0077	www.viromed.com	Microbiological	
White Eagle	2003 Lower State Rd. Camden, NJ	(215) 348-3868 (p)	www.latanet.com/e-source/!VENDORS.MZ/!WHITEEG.HTM	Yes	
Toxicology Labs	Doylestown, PA 18901	(215) 348 5081 (f)			
WIL Research Labs, Inc.	1407 George Rd. Ashland, OH 44805	(419) 289 8700 (p) / (419) 289 3650 (f)	www.wilresearch.com	Yes	SP, WL
XenoBiotics	Plainsboro, NJ	(609) 799-2295 / (609) 799-7497	www.xbl.com	Clinical	
Xenotech	Lenexa, Kansas	(913) 438-7450	www.xenotech.com	Yes	

- A "Yes" or "+" listed in the additional services column indicates that there are more services available than just those listed.
- SP in the special studies column indicates safety pharmacology, WL in this column indicates wildlife/environmental testing is available, EN in this column indicates that environmental testing in available.

Miscellaneous Labs
and Services

Vendor	Location	Phone #	Website	Pharmacology	Metabolism	Contract Device Manufacturing	Contract Sterilization	Physical Testing	Additional Services
ABC Laboratories	Columbia, MD	(573) 474-8579	www.abslabs.com					X	Manufacture, stability
AccuScan Testing, Inc.	Fort Worth, TX	(817) 478-4424	www.accuscantesting.com					X	
Advanced Polymers, Inc.	Salem, NH	(603) 898-8962	www.advpoly.com			X			
Aircom Manufacturing, Inc.	Indianapolis, IN	(800) 925-2426	www.aircommfg.com			X			Distribution
AMF Technologies	Boston, MA	(800) 998-0390	www.amftechnologies.com			X			Project management
ANPRO	Haw River, NC	(800) 523-1276	www.anpro.com				X		
ARC Specialty Product		(845) 355-5300	www.balchem.com/arc				X		
BAS	W. Lafayette, IN	(800) 845-4246 (765) 463-4527	www.bioanalytical.com					X	Method validation
BD Biosciences	Palo Alto, CA	(877) 232-8995	www.bdbiosciences.com	X					
Biolene	Buenos Aires, Argentina	+54 220 492 0506	www.biolene.com				X		
Biopharmaceutical Research Inc.	Vancouver, Canada	(604) 432-9237	www.bripharm.com	X					Stability, label, QA, QC
Calvert Preclinical	Olyphant, PA	(570) 586-2411	www.calvertpreclin.com	X	X				Pharmacokinetics, QA
Cardinal Health	Dublin, OH	(614) 757-5000	www.cardinal.com					X	Development, manufacturing, stability
Case Medical	Ridgefield, NJ	(888) 227-CASE	www.casemed.com				X		
Cecon Consulting Group	Wilmington, DE	(302) 994-8000	www.cecon.com					X	
Charles River Laboratories	Worchester, MA Redfield, AR Reno, NV Horsham, PA Spencerville, OH	(978) 658-6000 (877) 274-8371 (419) 647-4196	www.criver.com	X					Manufacture

Company	Location	Phone	Website	Services
Chemir	Maryland Heights, MO	(314) 291-6620	www.chemir.com	Validation
Chesapeake Biological Labs	Baltimore, MD	(800) 441-4225	www.cblinc.com	Validation
Chromak Research, Inc.	Somerset, NJ	(800) 563-9964	N/A	Stability, clinical design & management, consulting
Cosmed Group, Inc.	Jamestown, RI	(401) 423-2003	www.cosmedgroup.com	
Covance	Princeton, NJ	(888) COVANCE	www.covance.com	Method validation, analysis
CTBR	Quebec, Canada	(514) 630-8200	www.ctbr.com	Development, consulting
CXRbiosciences	Scotland, UK	+44 (0) 1382 432163	www.cxrbiosciences.com	
Dalton Chemical Laboratories, Inc.	Toronto, ON	(800) 567-5060	www.dalton.com	Scale up, development
DEKA Research and Development Corporation	Manchester, NH	(603) 669-5139	www.dekaresearch.com	Design
Drug Safety Eval. Consulting, Inc.	Birmingham, AL	(205) 995-9545	www.dseconsulting.com	Stability, method validation
Eclipse Scientific Group	Cambridgeshire, UK	01354 695858	www.eclipsescientific.co.uk	Method development, stability
ETC Sterilization Systems	Southampton, PA	(215) 355-9100	www.etcsterization.com	
Ethox Corp.	Buffalo, NY	(716) 842-4000	www.ethoxcorp.com	
Exygen Research	State College, PA	(800) 281-3219	www.exygen.com	Method validation, Chem. analysis, stability
Galbraith	Knoxville, TN	(865) 546-1335	www.galbraith.com	Design, testing
Geneva Medical Products, LLC	Walworth, WI	(866) 383-3323	www.genevamedical.com	
Gwathmey, Inc.	Cambridge, MA	(617) 491-0022 ext22	www.gwathmey.com	Consulting
Huntingdon Life Sciences Group plc	England	+44 148-089-2000	www.huntingdon.com	Phase II, III
IBA	CA, IL, OH, TX, NC, NJ, MD, AK, GA, NM, NY, UT		www.iba-worldwide.com	
IMI (TAMI)	Haifa Bay, Israel	972-4-8469411	www.tami-imi.com	Development
In Vitro Technologies	Baltimore, MD	(410) 455-1245	www.invitrotech.com	Validation
INA Research Inc.	Japan Philippines	0265-72-6616	www.ina-research.co.jp	Consulting

Vendor	Location	Phone #	Website	Pharmacology	Metabolism	Contract Device Manufacturing	Contract Sterilization	Physical Testing	Additional Services
Innoventor Engineering, Inc.	Maryland Heights, MO	(314) 692-9998	www.innoventor.net			X			
Inveresk Research	Scotland	+44 (0) 1875 614545	www.inversek.com	X					Validation, phase II, III, IV, stability, storage, inhalation
Isomedix	Mentor, OH	(888) 8STERIS	www.steris.com/isomedix				X		
Isotron	Wiltshire, UK	+44 (0) 1793 601006	www.isotron.co.uk				X		
ITR Laboratories Canada Inc.	Quebec, Canada	(514) 457-7400	www.itrlab.com	X					Method validation, development
LAB	Quebec, Canada	(450) 973-2240	www.preclin.com	X					Method validation
Lake Region Manufacturing	Chaska, MN	(800) DIAL LRM	www.lakergn.com			X			
LBR Scientific, Inc.	Clifton, NJ	(973) 473-0039	Lbrscientific.com					X	
Magellan Labs	RTP, NC	(919) 481-4855	www.magellanlabs.com					X	Stability, validation
MedSource Technologies Portlyn	Moultonboro, NH	(603) 476-5538	www.medsourcetech.com			X			Design
Meridian Medical Technologies, Inc.	Columbia, MD	(800) 638-8093	www.meridianmeds.com			X		X	Validation, develop
Metal Chem Industries	Mumbai	5773780	www.metalchemindia.com			X		X	
Metrics, Inc.	Greenville, NC	(252) 752-3800	www.metricsinc.com	X					Validation, storage
Microbac	Erie, PA / Hampton, VA	(814) 833-5672 / (757) 826-8262	www.microbac.com					X	
Micro-Med Inc.	Portsmouth, NH	(603) 427-5511	N/A			X			Packaging
Midwest Research Institute	Kansas City, MO	(816) 753-7600	www.mriresearch.org	X	X				Method validation
MPI Research	Mattawan, Michigan	(616) 668-3336	www.mpiresearch.com	X	X				Inhalation

Company	Location	Phone	Website	Col1	Col2	Col3	Col4	Services
NASP	Franklin, NJ	(373) 290-4388	www.naspco.com	X				Phase I, II, pharmacokinetics, QA
Northwest Kinetics, L.L.C.	Tacoma, WA	(253) 593-5304	www.nwkinetics.com	X				
Nucro Technics	Scarborough, Ontario	(416) 438-6727	www.nucro.com	X				Phase II, III, IV, method validation
NUTEK	Hayward, CA	(510) 429-2900	www.nutekcorp.com		X			Package, QA, stability, validation
OSG Norwich Pharmaceuticals	Norwich, NY	(607) 335-3000	www.norwichpharma.com		X			
Packaging Coordinators Inc.	Philadelphia, PA	(215) 637-8100	N/A					
Pall Life Sciences	East Hills, NY	(800) 717-7255	www.pall.com/biopharmaceutical	X				Validation, liquids
PAREXEL Intl. Corp.	Boston, MA	(781) 487-9900	www.parexel.com	X				Phase II, III, IV, validation
Pathology Associates	Frederick, MD	(301) 663-1644	www.paicriver.com	X	X			Software
	Durham, NC	(919) 544-5257						
Patrick Plastics Corp.	West Chicago, IL	(630) 639-5011	www.patrickplastics.com		X			
PCI Services	Philadelphia, PA	(215) 637-8100	www.pciservices.com	X				Manufacture, package, validation
Pharmaceutical Development Center	Charleston, SC	(843) 746-2500	www.pdclabs.com		X			
PPD, Inc.	Austin, TX	(512) 5819156	www.ppdi.com	X				QA, QC, pharmacokinetics
Primus	Omaha, NE	(402) 344-4206	www.primus-sterilizer.com	X		X		
QTI	Whitehouse, NJ	(908) 534-4455	www.QTIonline.com	X				Validation, stability, consulting
Quality Chemical Laboratories	Wilmington, NC	(910) 796-3441	www.qualitychemlabs.com	X				Development, validation, stability
Quest Pharmaceutical Services, L.L.C.	Newark, DE	(302) 369-5601	www.questpharm.com	X				Validation
Quintiles	Kansas City, MO	(816) 767-3900	www.quintiles.com	X				Package, manufacture
	RTP, NC	(877) 988-2100		X				
RCC	Switzerland	+41 61 975 11 11	www.rcc.ch	X				Inhalation, phase II, III
Resonetics, Inc.	Nashua, NH	(603) 886-6772	www.resonetics.com		X			
Ricerca	Concord, OH	(888) 763-4797	www.ricerca.com	X				Development, manufacture
Ruhof	Mineola, NY	(516) 294-5888	www.ruhof.com				X	
Saphikon Inc.	Milford, NH	(800) 899-5831	www.saphikon.com		X			
Source Precision Medicine	Boulder, CO	(303) 385-2700	www.sourcemedicine.com	X				Genomic outsourcing
Southern BioSystems, Inc.	Birmingham, AL	(877) 917-2200	www.southernbiosystems.com	X				

Vendor	Location	Phone #	Website	Pharmacology	Metabolism	Contract Device Manufacturing	Contract Sterilization	Physical Testing	Additional Services
Southern Research Institute	Birmingham, AL	(888) 322-1166 (205) 322-7472	www.southernresearch.com	X					Cancer, phase II, III
SRI International	Menlo Park, CA	(650) 859-4771	www.sri.com	X	X				
Star Services, Inc.	Hayward, CA	(510) 782-8848	www.starservicesinc.com				X		QC, QA
Sterile Technologies	Queensbury, NY	(518) 793-7677	www.steriletech.com				X	X	
Sterilization Services, Inc.	Atlanta, GA	(404) 344-8423	www.sterilization-services.com				X	X	
Stimtech, Inc.	Amherst, NH	(603) 880-5050	www.stimtech.com			X			
STS	Henrietta, NY	(800) 836-4850	www.stsduotek.com			X	X		Distribution
TFX Medical Incorporated	Jaffrey, NH	(603) 532-7706	www.tfxmedical.com			X	X		
Titan Scan Technologies	San Diego, CA	(858) 812-6514	www.titanscan.com				X		
Tower Laboratories	Centerbrook, CT	(888) 22TOWER	www.towerlabs.com			X			Packaging
U. of Iowa Div. of Pharm. Science	Iowa City, IA	(319) 335-8674 (319) 335-4096	www.uiowa.edu/~pharmaser www.uiowa.edu/~cadd	X					Method validation
Vacudyne	Chicago Heights, IL	(708) 757-5200	www.vacudyne.com				X	X	
Ventrex, Inc.	Ventura, CA	(805) 658-2984	www.ventrexinc.com				X	X	
Vetter	Ranesburg, Germany	49-751-3700-0	www.vetter-group.com	X					Aseptically pre-filled applications, package, stability, validation
Vital Pharma Inc.	Riviera Beach, FL	(561) 844-3221	www.vitalpharma.com			X			Validation, stability
WellSpring Pharmaceutical	Oakville, ON	(866) 337-4500	www.wellspringpharm.com/ contractservices/wellspring.html		X				

Analytical Labs

Vendor	Location	Phone #	Website	Analytical	Bioanalytical	Additional Services
AAI	Wilmington, NC	(910) 254-7000	www.aaiintl.com	X	X	Method validation, project management
Abbott	Abbott Park, IL	(847) 935-0945	www.abbottcontractmfg.com	X		Delivery
ABC Laboratories	Columbia, MD	(573) 474-8579	www.abslabs.com	X	X	Manufacture, stability
Alpharma	Baltimore, MD	(410) 277-1301	Alpharmauspd.com	X		Packaging, liquid & topical
Alturas Analytics Inc.	Moscow, ID	(208) 883-3400	www.alturasanalytics.com	X	X	Pharmacokinetics, validation
Applied Analytical Industries, Inc.	Wilmington, NC	(800) 575-4224	www.aaiintl.com	X	X	Validation, phase II, III, IV, stability
Atlantic Pharm. Services	Owing Mills, MD	(410) 413-1000	www.apsoutsource.com	X		
BAS	W. Lafayette, IN	(800) 845-4246 (765) 463-4527	www.bioanalytical.com	X	X	Method validation
Battelle	Columbus, OH	(800) 201-2011	www.battelle.org	X		Toxicology lab
Baxter	Bloomington, IN	(800) 353-0887	www.baxterdrugdelivery.com	X		Stability, packaging
Biopharmaceutical Research Inc.	Vancouver, Canada	(604) 432-9237	www.bripharm.com	X	X	Stability, label, QA, QC
BioReliance Corp.	Rockville, MD	(301) 738-1000	www.bioreliance.com	X		Manufacture, stability
Boston Analytical Inc.	Salem, NH	(603) 893-3758	www.bostonanalytical.com	X		Method validation, stability
BTC	Irvine, CA	(949) 660-3185	www.biologicaltestcenter.com	X		Toxicology lab
Calvert Preclinical	Olyphant, PA	(570) 586-2411	www.calvertpreclin.com	X		Toxicology lab, QA, pharmacokinetics
Celsis Lab Group	St. Louis, MO	(800) 523-5227	www.celsislabs.com	X		Method validation, stability, safety, efficacy
Central Toxicology Labs – Sygenta	UK	+44 16255 15852	N/A	X		Toxicology lab
Charles River Laboratories	Wilmington, MA	(978) 658-6000	www.criver.com	X	X	Manufacture
Chemir/Polytech Labs	Maryland Heights, MO	(800) 659-7659	www.chemir.com	X		Development, validation, stability
CIT	Evreux, France	+33 2 32 292626	www.citox.com	X	X	Toxicology lab, validation
Covance	Princeton, NJ	(888) COVANCE	www.covance.com	X	X	Stability, clinical design & management, consulting
CPT Co.	Fairfield, NJ	(973) 808-7111	www.cptlabs.com	X		Method validation, stability, product testing

Company	Location	Phone	Website			Services
CTBR	Quebec, Canada	(514) 630-8200	www.ctbr.com	X	X	Method validation, analysis
Dow Chemical	Midland, MI	(800) 304-1488	www.dowcms.com	X		Excipients, manufacture
DPT	Smithfield, RI; San Antonio, TX	(866) CALL DPT	www.dptlabs.com	X		Manage, produce, compounding, package
Drug Safety Eval. Consulting, Inc.	Birmingham, AL	(205) 995-9545	www.dseconsulting.com		X	Stability, method validation
DSM Catalytica Pharmaceutical	Greenville, NC	(252) 707-2307	www.dsmcatalytica-pharm.com	X		Method validation, stability
Elite Labs	Northvale, NJ	(201) 750-2646	www.elitepharma.com	X		Manufacture
Enviro Biotech	Bernville, PA	(610) 488-7664	N/A	X		Environmental, method validation, stability, chicken, cow
Exygen Research	State College, PA	(800) 281-3219	www.exygen.com	X	X	Method validation, Chem. analysis, stability
Fraunhofer ITA	Hannover, Germany	+49 511 5353 0	www.ita.fhg.com	X		Toxicology lab
Galbraith Labs, Inc.	Knoxville, TN	(877) 449-8797	www.galbraith.com	X		Environmental, method validation
Glatt Contract Services	Ramsey, NJ	(201) 825-8700	www.glattair.com	X		Validation
Hollister-Stier	Spokane, WA	(800) 992-1120	www.hollister-stier.com	X		Label, package, project management, validation
ILS	RTP, NC	(919) 544-5857	www.ils-inc.com	X		QA
In Vitro Technologies	Baltimore, MD	(410) 455-1245	www.invitrotech.com	X	X	Validation
Inveresk Research	Scotland	+44 (0) 1875 614545	www.inversek.com	X	X	Validation, phase II, III, IV, stability, storage, inhalation
Irvine Analytical Laboratories, Inc.	Irvine, CA	(877) 445-6554	www.ialab.com	X		Validations, inhalation, QC, environmental
Irysis	San Diego, CA	(858) 623-1520	www.irisys.com	X		Liquid-filled capsules, peptides, proternal, organics
Kendle Intl. Inc.	Cincinnati, OH	(513) 381-5550	www.kendle.com		X	Software, validation, project management
Lancaster Labs	Lancaster, PA	(717) 656-2300	www.lancasterlabs.com	X	X	Stability, validation
Lyne Labs	Brockton, MA	(800) 525-0450	www.lyne.com	X		Manufacture, stability, package
Magellan Labs	RTP, NC	(919) 481-4855	www.magellanlabs.com	X	X	Stability, validation
Maxxam Analytics Inc.	Toronto, Canada; Calgary, Canada; Montreal, Canada; Edmonton, Can.	(905) 890-2555; (403) 291-3077; (514) 636-6218; (780) 468-3500	www.maxxam.ca	X	X	Phase II, III, IV

Vendor	Location	Phone #	Website	Analytical	Bioanalytical	Additional Services
McKesson	Rockville, MD	(888) 4-MBS-BIO	www.mckessonbio.com	X		Clinical management, package, label, store
MDS	Quebec, Canada	(514) 333-0033	www.mdsps.com	X	X	Management
MediChem	Woodridge, IL	(630) 783-4600	www.medichem.com	X	X	Development, project management
Medtox Laboratories Inc.	St. Paul, MN	(800) 832-3244	www.medtox.com		X	Phase II, III, IV, QC, QA
Metrics, Inc.	Greenville, NC	(252) 752-3800	www.metricsinc.com	X		Validation, storage
Micron Tech	Exton, PA	(610) 425-5100	www.microntech.com	X		Particle size reduction, QH
Midwest Research Institute	Kansas City, MO	(816) 753-7600	www.mriresearch.org	X		Method validation
MiKart	Atlanta, GA	(404) 351-4510	www.mikart.com	X		Validation, stability, package
Northview Biosciences	Spartanburg, SC / Northbrook, IL / Berkeley, CA	(864) 574-7728 / (847) 564-8181 / (510) 548-8440	www.northviewlabs.com	X		Biocompatability, validation
Nucro Technics	Scarborough, Ontario	(416) 438-6727	www.nucro.com	X		Phase II, III, IV, method validation
OctoPlus	Netherlands	+31 (71) 524 40 44	www.octoplus.nl	X		QC
Omnicare	King of Prussia, PA	(800) 290-5766	www.omnicarecr.com	X		Project management, consulting, package
OSG Norwich	Norwich, NY	(607) 335-3000	www.norwichpharma.com	X		Manufacture, package, QV, QC, validation
Pall Life Sciences	East Hills, NY	(800) 717-7255	www.pall.com/biopharmaceutical	X		Validation, liquids
Patheon	Ontario, Canada	(888) PATHEON	www.patheon.com	X	X	Manufacture, many dosage forms
Pathology Associates	Frederick, MD / Durham, NC	(301) 663-1644 / (919) 544-5257	www.paicriver.com	X	X	Software
PCI Services	Philadelphia, PA	(215) 637-8100	www.pciservices.com	X		Manufacture, package, validation
Pharm Eco	North Andover, MA	(978) 784-5000	www.pharmeco.com	X		Manufacture, development
Pharma Medica	Ontario, Canada	(905) 624-9115 / (877) PHARMA1	www.pharmamedica.com	X	X	Phase II, III, IV, development, validation
Pharmacia	Kalamazoo, MI	(616) 833-5844	www.pharmaciacentresource.com	X		Manufacture
PharmaKinetics Laboratories Inc.	Baltimore, MD	(410) 385-4500	www.pharmakinetics.com		X	Phase III, IV

Company	Location	Phone	Website			Services
Pharmatek	San Diego, CA	(858) 350-8789	www.pharmatek.com	X		Pharma chem., small peptides
Pion	Wodburn, MA	(781) 935-8939	www.pion-inc.com	X		pka
Pisgah Labs Inc.	Pisgah Forest, NC	(828) 884-2789	www.pisgahlabs.com	X		Validation, manufacture
PPD, Inc.	Austin, TX	(512) 5819156	www.ppdi.com	X	X	QA, QC, pharmacokinetics
Product Safety Labs	Dayton, New Jersey	(732) 438-5100	www.productsafetylabs.com	X		Method development
QTI	Whitehouse, NJ	(908) 534-4455	www.QTIonline.com	X		Validation, stability, consulting
Quality Chemical Laboratories	Wilmington, NC	(910) 796-3441	www.qualitychemlabs.com	X		Development, validation, stability
Quest Pharmaceutical Services, L.L.C.	Newark, DE	(302) 369-5601	www.questpharm.com	X	X	Validation
Quintiles	Kansas City, MO / RTP, NC	(816) 767-3900 / (877) 988-2100	www.quintiles.com	X	X	Package, manufacture
RCC	Switzerland	+41 61 975 11 11	www.rcc.ch	X		Inhalation, phase II, III
Ricerca	Concord, OH	(888) 763-4797	www.ricerca.com	X	X	Development, manufacture
RTI	RTP, NC	(919) 541-6000	www.rti.com	X		Toxicology lab
SafePharm	Derby, UK	00 44 (0) 1332 792896	www.safepharm.com	X		Toxicology lab
Sequani	UK	+44 (0) 1531 634121	www.sequani.com	X		QA, program management
SGS	Fairfield, NJ	(800) 777-8278	www.ustesting.sgsna.com	X		Toxicology lab
Siegfried Actives	Pennsville, NJ / Switzerland	(877) 763-8630 / +44 62 746 1212	www.siegfried.ch	X		QC, QA
Siegfried Exclusives	Pennsville, NJ / Switzerland	(856) 678-3601 / +41 62 746 1221	www.siegfried.ch	X		Storage, QC, QA
Siegfried Ventures	San Diego, CA / Pennsville, NJ / Switzerland	(858) 546-4346 / (856) 678-3809 / +41 62 746 1111	www.siegfried.ch	X		QC, QA
SL Pharma Labs	Wilmington, DE	(302) 636-0202	www.slpharmalabs.com	X		Method validation, stability, development
SNBL USA Ltd	Everett, WA	(425) 407-0121	www.snblusa.com	X		QA
Source Precision Medicine	Boulder, CO	(303) 385-2700	www.sourcemedicine.com	X	X	Genomics outsourcing
Southern Research Institute	Birmingham, AL	(888) 322-1166 / (205) 322-7472	www.southernresearch.com	X	X	Cancer, phase II, III
Southern Testing & Research Labs	Wilson, NC	(252) 237-4175	www.southerntesting.com	X		Development, validation, stability
SPIbio	France	33 (0) 169 53 14 00	www.spibio.com	X		Toxicology lab
SRI International	Menlo Park, CA	(650) 859-4771	www.sri.com	X		QC, QA

Vendor	Location	Phone #	Website	Analytical	Bioanalytical	Additional Services
Stiefel Research Institute	Oak Hill, NY	(800) 633-7647	www.stiefelresearch.com	X		Topicals, development, validation
Stillmeadow Incorporated	Sugar Land, TX	(281) 240-8828	www.stillmeadow.com	X		Inhalation, stability, method validation
STS duoTEK, Inc.	Rush, NY	(800) 836-4850	www.stsduotek.com	X		Stability, microbiology, package
TNO Pharma	The Netherlands	+31 30 694 4806	www.pharma.tno.nl	X		Toxicology lab
Toxicology Research Laboratory	Chicago, IL	(312) 996-9185	N/A	X		
U. Pharmaceuticals of Maryland, Inc.	St. Baltimore, MD	(410) 843-3700	www.upm-inc.com	X		SUPAC Guidance, training
Viromed Laboratories	Minneapolis, MN	(800) 582-0077	www.viromed.com	X		QA
	St. Paul, MN	(800) 582-0077				
	Marietta, GA	(888) 847-6633				
	Camden, NJ	(800) 622-8820				
Vital Pharma Inc.	Riviera Beach, Florida	(561) 844-3221	www.vitalpharma.com	X		Validation
West Pharmaceutical Service	Lionville, PA	(610) 594-2900	www.westpharma.com	X		Device & package components, drug-package, interactions
Yamanouchi Pharma	Norman, OK	(888) 236-5553	www.ypharma.com	X		Manufacture, validation, stability, solid dose

APPENDIX

GMP Contract Facilities

Vendor	Location	Phone #	Website	CGMP Synthesis	Synthesis of Radiolabeled Compound	Biologic Product Manufacture	Additional Services
ABC Laboratories	Columbia, MD	(573) 474-8579	www.abslabs.com	X	X		Manufacture, stability
Accucaps	Ontario, Canada	(800) 665-7210	www.accucaps.com	X			Validation
Akorn	Decatur, IL	(800) 810-8170	www.akorn.com	X			Solutions, ointments, delivery, manufacture
Almedica	Alendale, NJ	(888) 4-ALMEDICA	www.almedica.com	X			Labels, package, project management
American Radiolabeled Chemicals	St. Louis, MO	(314) 991-4545	www.arc-inc.com		X		
Amersham Biosciences	Piscataway, NJ / Freiburg, Germany / Tokyo, Japan	(732) 457-8000 / +49 (0)761 4903 0 / +81 3 5331 9383	www.amershambiosciences.com	X	X		
Atlantic Pharm. Services	Owing Mills, MD	(410) 413-1000	www.apsoutsource.com	X			
BAS	W. Lafayette, IN	(800) 845-4246 / (765) 463-4527	www.bioanalytical.com	X			Method validation
Boehringer Ingelheim Promeco	Mexico	(5255) 5629 8300	www.boehringer-ingelheim.com	X			Validation
Cambrex Bio Science	Baltimore, MD	(410) 563-9200	www.bscp.com	X			Development, QC, QA, validation
Cangene Corp.	Winnipeg, Canada	(204) 275-4200	www.cangene.com	X			Label & packaging
Charles River Laboratories	Wilmington, MA	(978) 658-6000	www.criver.com	X			Manufacture
Chem Syn	Lenexa, KY	(800) 233-6643	www.chemsyn.com	X	X		Processing, method validation
Chromos Molecular Systems Inc.	Burnaby, BC, Canada	(604) 415-7100	www.chromos.com			X	
ConjuChem Inc.	Quebec, Canada	(514) 844-5558	www.conjuchem.com			X	
Covalent Group Inc.	Wayne, PA	(610) 975-9533	www.covalentgroup.com	X			Consulting, project management, QA
Covance	Quebec, Canada	(514) 421-8150	www.covance.com			X	

Company	Location	Phone	Website			Services
CPL	Ontario, Canada	(905) 821-7600	www.cplltd.com	X		Oral & topical, package, manufacture
CQ1-Biomed International Inc.	Quebec, Canada	(450) 443-6011			X	
Cronus BioPharma Inc.	Winnipeg, Canada	(204) 477-1611			X	
CV Technologies	Edmonton, Canada	(780) 432-0022	www.cvtechnologies.com		X	
Cytochroma Inc.	Ontario, Canada	(613) 531-9995	www.cytochroma.com		X	
Cytovax Biotechnologies Inc.	Edmonton, Canada	(780) 448-0621	www.cytovax.com		X	
Dalton Chemical Laboratories Inc.	Toronto, Canada	(416) 661-2102	www.dalton.com		X	
Diabetogen Biosciences Inc.	Ontario, Canada	(519) 858-5186	www.diabetogen.com		X	
Dimethaid Research Inc.	Ontario, Canada	(905) 415-1446	www.dimethaid.com		X	Stability, scale-up
Diosynth	RTP, NC	(919) 468-9400	www.diosynth.com	X		
Dominion Biologicals Limited	Dartmouth, Canada	(902) 468-3992	www.immuncor.com		X	
Doosan Serdary Research Labs	Ontario, Canada	(416) 742-0774			X	
Dow Chemical	Midland, MI; Smithfield, RI	(800) 304-1488	www.dowcms.com	X		Excipients, manufacture
DRAXIS Health Inc.	Ontario, Canada	(905) 677-5500	www.draxis.com		X	
DSM Biologics Company Inc.	Quebec, Canada	(514) 341-9940	www.dsmbiologics.com		X	
DSM Catalytica Pharmaceutical	Greenville, NC	(252) 707-2307	www.dsmcatalytica-pharm.com	X		Method validation, stability
Ecopia BioSciences Inc.	Quebec, Canada	(514) 336-2700	www.ecopiabio.com		X	
Elitra Canada Ltd	Quebec, Canada	(514) 987-0415	www.elitra.com		X	
Ferro	Waukegan, IL	(847) 623-0370	www.pfanstiechl.com	X		Manufacture, method validation
Forbes Medi-Tech Inc.	Vancouver, Canada	(604) 689-5899	www.forbesmedi.com	X		Development, manufacturing
Formatech	Andover, MA	(877) 853-KEYS	www.formatech.com		X	
Fytokem Products Inc.	Saskatoon, Canada	(306) 668-2552	www.fytokem.com		X	
GB Therapeutics Ltd	Ontario, Canada	(613) 545-1239	www.gbtherapeutics.com		X	
Gelda Scientific & Indust. Dev. Corp.	Ontario, Canada	(905) 673-9320	www.gelda.com		X	

Vendor	Location	Phone #	Website	CGMP Synthesis	Synthesis of Radiolabeled Compound	Biologic Product Manufacture	Additional Services
Gemin X Biotechnologies Inc.	Quebec, Canada	(514) 281-8989	www.geminx.com			X	
GEMMA BioTechnology Ltd	Ontario, Canada	(519) 837-8862	www.gemmabiotech.com			X	
Generex Biotechnology Corp.	Ontario, Canada	(416) 364-2551	www.generex.com			X	
Genomics One Corporation	Quebec, Canada	(450) 688-4499	www.genomicsone.com			X	
GenSci Regeneration Sciences Inc.	Ontario, Canada	(800) 561-2955	www.gensci.bc.ca			X	
Genzyme Pharmaceuticals	Cambridge, MA	(800) 868-8208	www.genzyme.com/pharmaceuticals	X			Manufacture
Girindus	Cincinnati, OH	(513) 679-3000	www.girindus.com	X			QA, QA, radiochemistry
Glatt Contract Services	Ramsey, NJ	(201) 825-8700	www.glattair.com	X			Validation
GLYCODesign Inc.	Ontario, Canada	(416) 593-6027	www.glycodesign.com			X	
Haemacure Corp.	Quebec, Canada	(514) 282-3350	www.haemacure.com			X	
Hemosol Inc.	Ontario, Canada	(905) 286-6200	www.hemosol.com			X	
HyClone	Logan, UT	(800) 492-5663	www.hyclone.com	X			Liquids, single-use package
IBEX Pharmaceuticals Inc.	Quebec, Canada	(514) 334-4004	www.ibexpharma.ca			X	
Immune Network Corp. Comm. Ltd	Vancouver, Canada	(604) 222-5541	www.immunenetwork.com			X	
Inex Pharmaceuticals Corp.	Burnaby, BC, Canada	(604) 419-3200	www.inexpharm.com			X	
Lyne Labs	Brockton, MA	(800) 525-0450	www.lyne.com	X			Manufacture, stability, package
Magellan Labs	RTP, NC	(919) 481-4855	www.magellanlabs.com	X			Stability, validation
MDS Pharma Services	Quebec, Canada	(514) 333-0033	www.mdsps.com		X		
Medicago Inc.	Quebec, Canada	(418) 658-9393	www.medicago.com			X	Management

Company	Location	Phone	Website	Services
MediChem	Woodridge, IL	(630) 783-4600	www.medichem.com	Development, project management
Meridian Medical Technologies	Columbia, MD	(410) 309-6830	www.meridianmeds.com	Package
Microbix Biosystems Inc.	Ontario, Canada	(416) 234-1624	www.microbix.com	X
Midwest Research Institute	Kansas City, MO	(816) 753-7600	www.mriresearch.org	Method validation
Mova	Caguas, Puerto Rico	(800) 468-5201	www.movapharm.com	Manufacture, package
MRI Research	Kansas City, KS	(816) 753-7600	www.mriresearch.org	X
National Cancer Institute	Bethesda, MD	(800) 4-CANCER	www.nci.nih.gov	X
Neurochem Inc.	Quebec, Canada	(514) 337-4646	www.neurochem.com	X
NeuroMed Technologies Inc.	Vancouver, Canada	(604) 822-9970	www.neuromedtech.com	X
New Life Resources	Northvale, NJ	(201) 750-7880	www.newliferecources.net	Manufacture, hard-gel caps
Nexia Biotechnologies Inc.	Quebec, Canada	(450) 424-3067	www.nexiabiotech.com	X
Northview Biosciences	Spartanburg, SC / Northbrook, IL / Berkeley, CA	(864) 574-7728 / (847) 564-8181 / (510) 548-8440	www.northviewlabs.com	Biocompatability, validation
Nucro Technics	Scarborough, Ontario	(416) 438-6727	www.nucro.com	Phase II, III, IV, method validation
OctoPlus	The Netherlands	+31 (71) 524 40 44	www.octoplus.nl	QC
Oncolytics Biotech Inc.	Calgary, Canada	(403) 670-7377	www.onloyticsbiotech.com	X
OSG Norwich	Norwich, NY	(607) 335-3000	www.norwichpharma.com	Manufacture, package, QV, QC, validation
Pharm Eco	North Andover, MA	(978) 784-5000	www.pharmeco.com	Manufacture, development
Pharmacor Inc.	Quebec, Canada	(450) 973-1710	www.pharmacor.com	X
Pisgah Labs Inc.	Pisgah Forest, NC	(828) 884-2789	www.pisgahlabs.com	Validation, manufacture
PPD, Inc.	Austin, TX	(512) 5819156	www.ppdi.com	QA, QC, pharmacokinetics
Quality Chemical Laboratories	Wilmington, NC	(910) 796-3441	www.qualitychemlabs.com	Development, validation, stability
RTI International	RTP, NC	(919) 485-2666	www.rti.org	Radiochemistry, pharmacokinetics/toxicokinetics

Vendor	Location	Phone #	Website	CGMP Synthesis	Synthesis of Radiolabeled Compound	Biologic Product Manufacture	Additional Services
RusGen	Moscow, Russia	007-095-253-92-36	www.rusgen.com		X		
Sequani	UK	+44 (0) 1531 634121	www.sequani.com	X			QA, program management
Siegfried Actives	Pennsville, NJ Switzerland	(877) 763-8630 +44 62 746 1212	www.siegfried.ch	X			QC, QA
Siegfried Exclusives	Pennsville, NJ Switzerland	(856) 678-3601 +41 62 746 1221	www.siegfried.ch	X			Storage, QC, QA
Siegfried Ventures	San Diego, CA Pennsville, NJ Switzerland	(858) 546-4346 (856) 678-3809 +41 62 746 1111	www.siegfried.ch	X			QC, QA
Sigma-Aldrich	St. Louis, MO	(800) 336-9719	www.sigma-aldrich.com/safe	X			Manufacture
Southern Research Institute	Birmingham, AL	(888) 322-1166 (205) 322-7472	www.southernresearch.com	X			Cancer, phase II, III
Stiefel Research Institute	Oak Hill, NY	(800) 633-7647	www.stiefelresearch.com	X			Topicals, development, validation
U. of Iowa Div. of Pharm. Science	Iowa City, IA	(319) 335-8674 (319) 335-4096	www.uiowa.edu/~pharmaser www.uiowa.edu/~cadd	X			Method validation
Univ. of Rhode Island	Kingston, RI	(401) 874-5842	http://www.uri.edu/pharmacy/		X		
Viromed Laboratories	Minneapolis, MN St. Paul, MN Marietta, GA Camden, NJ	(800) 582-0077 (800) 582-0077 (888) 847-6633 (800) 622-8820	www.viromed.com	X			QA
Viron Therapeutics Inc.	Ontario, Canada	(519) 858-5109	www.vironinc.com			X	
Vital Pharma Inc.	Riviera Beach, Florida	(561) 844-3221	www.vitalpharma.com	X			Validation
Yale Pharmaceutical Research Institute	New Haven, CT	(301) 571-2388	http://www.yalepharma.com/ADME.htm	X	X		QA, QC, development

Formulation

APPENDIX

E

Vendor	Location	Phone #	Website	Formulation	Additional Services
AAI	Wilmington, NC	(910) 254-7000	www.aaiintl.com	X	Method validation, project management
Accucaps	Ontario, Canada	(800) 665-7210	www.accucaps.com	X	Validation
Akorn	Decatur, IL	(800) 810-8170	www.akorn.com	X	Solutions, ointments, delivery, manufacture
Alpharma	Baltimore, MD	(410) 277-1301	Alpharmauspd.com	X	Packaging, liquid & topical
Applied Analytical Industries, Inc.	Wilmington, NC	(800) 575-4224	www.aaiintl.com	X	Validation, phase II, III, IV, stability
Atlantic Pharm. Services	Owing Mills, MD	(410) 413-1000	www.apsoutsource.com	X	
BAS	W. Lafayette, IN	(800) 845-4246 (765) 463-4527	www.bioanalytical.com	X	Method validation
Baxter	Bloomington, IN	(800) 353-0887	www.baxterdrugdelivery.com	X	Stability, packaging
Beckloff Associates, Inc.	Overland Park, KS	(913) 451-3955	www.beckloff.com	X	Development
Ben Venue Lab	Bedford, OH	(440) 232-3320	www.benvenue.com	X	Package, method validation, stability
Biacore	Piscataway, NJ	(732) 885-5618	www.biacore.com	X	
Boston Analytical Inc.	Salem, NH	(603) 893-3758	www.bostonanalytical.com	X	Method validation, stability
Cambrex Bio Science	Baltimore, MD	(410) 563-9200	www.bscp.com	X	QC, QA, validation
Cangene Corp.	Winnipeg, Canada	(204) 275-4200	www.cangene.com	X	Label & packaging
Celsis Lab Group	St. Louis, MO	(800) 523-5227	www.celsislabs.com	X	Method validation, stability, safety, efficacy
Charles River Laboratories	Wilmington, MA	(978) 658-6000	www.criver.com	X	Manufacture
Chem Syn	Lenexa, KY	(800) 233-6643	www.chemsyn.com	X	Process, method validation
CPL	Ontario, Canada	(905) 821-7600	www.cplltd.com	X	Oral & topical, package, manufacture
CPT Co.	Fairfield, NJ	(973) 808-7111	www.cptclabs.com	X	Method validation, stability, product testing
CSC	Spanish Fork, UT	(801) 794-2600	www.calscorp.com	X	
CTBR	Quebec, Canada	(514) 630-8200	www.ctbr.com	X	Method validation, analysis
Diosynth	RTP, NC	(919) 468-9400	www.diosynth.com	X	Stability, scale-up
Dow Chemical	Midland, MI / Smithfield, RI	(800) 304-1488	www.dowcms.com	X	Excipients, manufacture
DPT	San Antonio, TX	(866) CALL DPT	www.dptlabs.com	X	Management, production, compounding, package

Company	Location	Phone	Website		Services
DSM Catalytica Pharmaceutical	Greenville, NC	(252) 707-2307	www.dsmcatalytica-pharm.com	X	Method validation, stability
Elite Labs	Northvale, NJ	(201) 750-2646	www.elitepharma.com	X	Manufacture
Enviro Biotech	Bernville, PA	(610) 488-7664	N/A	X	Environmental, method validation, stability, chicken, cow
Exygen Research	State College, PA	(800) 281-3219	www.exygen.com	X	Method validation, chem. analysis, stability
Ferro	Waukegan, IL	(847) 623-0370	www.pfanstiechl.com	X	Manufacture, method validation
Formatech	Andover, MA	(877) 853-KEYS	www.formatech.com	X	Development, manufacture
Genzyme Pharmaceuticals	Cambridge, MA	(800) 868-8208	www.genzyme.com/pharmaceuticals	X	Manufacture
Glatt Contract Services	Ramsey, NJ	(201) 825-8700	www.glattair.com	X	Validation
Inveresk Research	Scotland	+44 (0) 1875 614545	www.inveresk.com	X	Validation, phase II, III, IV, stability, storage, inhalation
Irvine Analytical Laboratories, Inc.	Irvine, CA	(877) 445-6554	www.ialab.com	X	Validations, inhalation, QC, environmental
Irysis	San Diego, CA	(858) 623-1520	www.irisys.com	X	Liquid-filled capsules, peptides, proternal, organics
Lyne Labs	Brockton, MA	(800) 525-0450	www.lyne.com	X	Manufacture, stability, package
Magellan Labs	RTP, NC	(919) 481-4855	www.magellanlabs.com	X	Stability, validation
Matrix Contract Services	San Diego, CA	(858) 824-5122	www.mtx.com	X	Filling, QC, validation, cancer
Meridian Medical Technologies	Columbia, MD	(410) 309-6830	www.meridianmeds.com	X	Package
Metrics, Inc.	Greenville, NC	(252) 752-3800	www.metricsinc.com	X	Validation, storage
Midwest Research Institute	Kansas City, MO	(816) 753-7600	www.mriresearch.org	X	Method validation
MiKart	Atlanta, GA	(404) 351-4510	www.mikart.com	X	Validation, stability, package
Miza	Toronto, Ontario	(416) 927-0600	www.miza.com	X	Stability, validation, manufacture
Molecular Medicine Bio Services, Inc.	San Diego, CA	(858) 523-9544	www.molecularmed.com	X	Cell & gene based therapeutics & vaccines, scale-up
OctoPlus	Netherlands	+31 (71) 524 40 44	www.octoplus.nl	X	QC
Pall Life Sciences	East Hills, NY	(800) 717-7255	www.pall.com/biopharmaceutical	X	Validation, liquids
Patheon	Ontario, Canada	(888) PATHEON	www.patheon.com	X	Manufacture, many dosage forms
Pharmaceutics International, Inc.	Hunt Valley, MD	(410) 584-0001	www.pharm-int.com	X	Packaging, project management, stability
Pharmatek	San Diego, CA	(858) 350-8789	www.pharmatek.com	X	Pharma chem., small peptides
Proclinical Pharmaceutical Services, Inc.	Phoenixville, PA	(610) 935-4300	www.proclinical.com	X	Packaging, stability

Vendor	Location	Phone #	Website	Formulation	Additional Services
Quintiles	Kansas City, MO RTP, NC	(816) 767-3900 (877) 988-2100	www.quintiles.com	X	Package, manufacture
Sigma-Aldrich	St. Louis, MO	(800) 336-9719	www.sigma-aldrich.com/safe	X	Manufacture
SNBL USA Ltd	Everett, WA	(425) 407-0121	www.snblusa.com	X	QA
Southern Research Institute	Birmingham, AL	(888) 322-1166 (205) 322-7472	www.southernresearch.com	X	Cancer, phase II, III
SRI International	Menlo Park, CA	(650) 859-4771	www.sri.com	X	Pharmacokinetics, QC, QA
Stiefel Research Institute	Oak Hill, NY	(800) 633-7647	www.stiefelresearch.com	X	Topicals, development, validation
U. of Iowa Div. of Pharm. Science	Iowa City, IA	(319) 335-8674 (319) 335-4096	www.uiowa.edu/~pharmaser www.uiowa.edu/~cadd	X	Method validation
U. Pharmaceuticals of Maryland, Inc.	?, MD	(410) 843-3700	www.upm-inc.com	X	SUPAC guidance, training
Vital Pharma Inc.	Riviera Beach, Florida	(561) 844-3221	www.vitalpharma.com	X	Validation
Yamanouchi Pharma	Norman, OK	(888) 236-5553	www.ypharma.com	X	Manufacture, validation, stability, solid dose

Dosage Forms

Vendor	Location	Phone #	Website	CTM	Label	Additional Services
AAI	Wilmington, NC	(910) 254-7000	www.aaiintl.com	X		Method validation, project management
ADL	UK	+44 (0) 1189 732525	www.labelaplicators.com		X	Solutions, ointments, delivery, manufacture
Akorn	Decatur, IL	(800) 810-8170	www.akorn.com		X	
Almedica	Alendale, NJ	(888) 4-ALMEDICA	www.almedica.com	X	X	Package, project management
ALTCO	Woodbridge, NJ	(732) 283-2722	Altco.com		X	
Applied Analytical Industries, Inc.	Wilmington, NC	(800) 575-4224	www.aaiintl.com	X		Validation, phase II, III, IV, stability
ARC	St. Louis, MO	(314) 991-4545	www.arc-inc.com	X		
Biopharmaceutical Research Inc.	Vancouver, Canada	(604) 432-9237	www.bripharm.com	X	X	Stability, QA, QC
Cangene Corp.	Winnipeg, Canada	(204) 275-4200	www.cangene.com	X	X	Packaging
CATO Research	Durham, NC	(919) 361-CATO	www.cato.com	X	X	
CCL Label	Framingham, MA	(508) 872-4511	www.cclind.com	X	X	
Chem Syn	Lenexa, KY	(800) 233-6643	www.chemsyn.com	X	X	Process, method validation
DaVita Inc.	Minneapolis, MN	(612) 347-6367	www.davitaresearch.com	X	X	Phase II, III, IV
Diosynth	RTP, NC	(919) 468-9400	www.diosynth.com	X	X	Stability, scale-up
Dow	Petaluma, CA	(707) 793-2600	www.dowpharm.com		X	
DSM Catalytica Pharmaceutical	Greenville, NC	(252) 707-2307	www.dsmcatalytica-pharm.com	X		Method validation, stability
Elite labs	Northvale, NJ	(201) 750-2646	www.elitepharma.com	X	X	Manufacture
EMMCORP	Hempstead, NY	(800) 835-2393	www.easternmarking.com		X	
FLEXcon	Spencer, MA	(508) 885-8200	www.flexcon.com		X	
Flottman Company	Crestview Hills, KY	(859) 331-6636	www.flottmanco.com		X	
Formatech	Andover, MA	(877) 853-KEYS	www.formatech.com	X		Development, manufacture
Girindus	Cincinnati, OH	(513) 679-3000	www.girindus.com	X		
Glatt Contract Services	Ramsey, NJ	(201) 825-8700	www.glattair.com	X		Validation
Hollister-Stier	Spokane, WA	(800) 992-1120	www.hollister-stier.com	X	X	Package, project management, validation

Company	Location	Phone	Website			Services
HyClone	Logan, UT	(800) 492-5663	www.hyclone.com	X		Liquids, single-use package
Irysis	San Diego, CA	(858) 623-1520	www.irisys.com	X		Liquid-filled capsules, peptides, proternal, organics
Labeltronix	Orange, CA	(800) 429-4321	www.labeltronix.com		X	
Lyne Labs	Brockton, MA	(800) 525-0450	www.lyne.com	X		Manufacture, stability, package
Magellan Laboratories	RTP, NC; Somerset, NJ; San Diego, CA; Albuquerque, NM	(919) 481-4855; (732) 302-1400; (858) 547-7800; (815) 338-9500	www.magellanlabs.com	X	X	Stability, validation
Matrix Contract Services	San Diego, CA	(858) 824-5122	www.matx.com	X		Filling, QC, validation, cancer
McKesson	Rockville, MD	(888) 4-MBS-BIO	www.mckessonbio.com		X	Clinical management, package, store
Meridian Medical Technologies	Columbia, MD	(410) 309-6830	www.meridianmeds.com	X		Package
Metrics, Inc.	Greenville, NC	(252) 752-3800	www.metricsinc.com	X		Validation, storage
Midwest Research Institute	Kansas City, MO	(816) 753-7600	www.mriresearch.org		X	Method validation
MiKart	Atlanta, GA	(404) 351-4510	www.mikart.com	X		Validation, stability, package
Molecular Medicine Bio Services, Inc.	San Diego, CA	(858) 523-9544	www.molecularmed.com	X		Cell & gene based therapeutics & vaccines, scale-up
Mova	Caguas, Puerto Rico	(800) 468-5201	www.movapharm.com	X		Manufacture, package
OSG Norwich	Norwich, NY	(607) 335-3000	www.norwichpharma.com	X		Manufacture, package, QV, QC, validation
Paragon Data Systems, Inc.	Cleveland, OH	(800) 211-0768	www.paragondatasystem.com		X	
Patheon	Ontario, Canada	(888) PATHEON	www.patheon.com	X		Manufacture, many dosage forms
PCI Services	Philadelphia, PA	(215) 637-8100	www.pciservices.com	X		Manufacture, package, validation
Pharmaceutical Research Company, Inc.	Exton, PA	(484) 875-9000	www.pharmaceuticalrc.com		X	
Pharmatek	San Diego, CA	(858) 350-8789	www.pharmatek.com	X		Pharma chem., small peptides
PPD, Inc.	Austin, TX	(512) 5819156	www.ppdi.com	X		QA, QC, pharmacokinetics
Quadrel Labeling Systems	Mentor, OH	(440) 602-4700	www.quadrel.com		X	Package, manufacture
Quintiles	Kansas City, MO; RTP, NC	(816) 767-3900; (877) 988-2100	www.quintiles.com	X		
RCC	Switzerland	+41 61 975 11 11	www.rcc.ch	X		Inhalation, phase II, III
Ricerca	Concord, OH	(888) 742-3722	www.ricerca.com		X	
Schwarz	Seymour, IN	(812) 523-5490	www.schwarzusa.com	X		Manufacture, package, support, method

Vendor	Location	Phone #	Website	Label CTM	Additional Services
Siegfried Exclusives	Pennsville, NJ / Switzerland	(856) 678-3601 / +41 62 746 1221	www.siegfried.ch	X	Storage, QC, QA
Southern Research Institute	Birmingham, AL	(888) 322-1166 / (205) 322-7472	www.southernresearch.com	X	Cancer, phase II, III
SRI International	Menlo Park, CA	(650) 859-4771	www.sri.com	X	Pharmacokinetics, QC, QA
Star Labeling Products	Fairless Hills, PA	(800) 394-6900	www.starlabel.com	X	
Stiefel Research Institute	Oak Hill, NY	(800) 633-7647	www.stiefelresearch.com	X	Topicals, development, validation
Tapecon	Buffalo, NY	(800) 333-2407	www.tapecon.com	X	
Taro	Hawthorne, NY	(800) 544-1449	www.tarousa.com	X	
TBCB	Garden Grove, CA	(714) 636-0561	www.pharmaceutical-equipment.com	X	
Toxcon	Edmonton, Can.	(780) 435-9028	www.toxcon.com	X	Risk assessment
U. of Iowa Div. of Pharm. Science	Iowa City, IA	(319) 335-8674 / (319) 335-4096	www.uiowa.edu/~pharmaser / www.uiowa.edu/~cadd	X	Method validation
U. Pharmaceuticals of Maryland, Inc.	St. Baltimore, MD	(410) 843-3700	www.upm-inc.com	X	SUPAC guidance, training

Clinical Testing

Vendor	Location	Phone #	Website	Clinical Support	Phase I Clinicals	Clinical Trial Management	Clinical Statistics	Additional Services
AACT	Cambridge, MA	(617) 520-3049	www.abtassociates.com				X	Project management, development
AAI	Wilmington, NC	(910) 254-7000	www.aaiintl.com		X	X	X	Method validation, project management
ABC.R.O	Washington, DC	(202) 234-6777	www.abcro.com		X			Project management, monitoring, phase II, III, IV
ABR	Pennington, NJ	(877) ABR-1001	www.abr-pharma.com		X			Phase II, III, IV
Abt Associates	Cambridge, MA	(617) 492-7100	www.abtassoc.com		X			
ACE Pharmaceuticals	The Netherlands	+31 (0) 36 5227201	www.ace-pharm.nl		X			Manufacture, package
ACM Medical Lab	Rochester, NY	(716) 247-3500	www.acmlab.com		X			Phase II, III, IV
Advanced Biologics	Lambertville, NJ	(609) 397-7891	www.advbiol.com			X		Programming, vaccine
Advanced Clinical Research	Salt Lake City, UT	(801) 355-4126	www.acr-research.com				X	
Advanced Clinical Services	Schaumburg, IL	(847) 995-9222	www.advancedclinical.com	X			X	Validation, programming
Algorithme Pharma	Laval, Quebec	(514) 858-6312	www.algopharm.com		X			QA
Almedica	Alendale, NJ	(888) 4-ALMEDICA	www.almedica.com			X		Package
Alquest	Minneapolis, MN	(877) 814-7529	www.alquest.com			X		
Applied Analytical Industries, Inc.	Wilmington, NC	(800) 575-4224	www.aaiintl.com		X			Validation, phase II, III, IV, stability
Applied Logic Associates, Inc.	Houston, TX	(713) 529-4747	www.alogic.com					
Araccel Corp.	Horsham, PA / Cary, NC	(215) 674-8174 / (919) 319-1404	www.araccel.com	X			X	Development, randomization
Arkios	Virginia Beach, VA	(757) 631-2114	www.arkios.com			X		QA
ARUP Labs	Salt Lake City, UT	(800) 242-2787	www.arup-lab.com		X			QA
Averion	Framingham, MA	(508) 416-2600	www.averioninc.com			X	X	Validation
Barton and Polansky Associates, Inc.	New York, NY	(212) 688-4343	www.bpa-mcs.com			X	X	QA/QC

Company	Location	Phone	Website	Services
BDH Clinical Research Services	Durham, NC	(919) 477-9542 x222	www.bdhclinical.com	QA
Beardsworth Consulting Group, Inc.	Flemington, NJ	(800) 788-6040	www.beardsworth.com	QA, phase IV, development
BioClin Health Research, Inc.	British Columbia, Canada	(604) 276-2580	www.bioclinresearch.com	
BioCor	Yardley, PA	(215) 321-9876	www.biocor.com	Programming, development, phase II, III, IV
BioSkin	Ashland, OR	+49 40 60 68 97 0	www.bioskin.com	
Biostat International, Inc.	Tampa, FL	(818) 979-1619	www.biostatinc.com	SAS, validation
Biotechnical Services, Inc.	North Little Rock, AR	(501) 758-6290	www.biotechnicalservices.com	Validation, programming, QA/QC
Brand Institute	Miami, FL	(305) 374-2500	www.brandinstitute.com	Validation
Buckman Co., Inc.	Pleasant Hill, CA	(925) 356-2640	www.fda-help.com	
CAP	Brookline, MA	(617) 713-4700	www.clinicalassistance.com	
Cardinal Systems	Paris, France	33 1 40 21 19 00	www.cardinal-sys.com	
Carolina Research Associates	Charlotte, NC	(704) 503-3216	Carolinaresearch.com	
CATO	Durham, NC	(919) 361-CATO	www.cato.com	Phase II, III, IV, monitoring
CEDRA Clinical Research	Austin, TX	(512) 345-7766	www.cedracorp.com	QA, development
Celeris Corporation	Nashville, TN	(615) 341-0223	www.celeriscorp.com	PLA prep
Cenetron	Austin, TX	(888) 834-6632	www.cenetron.com	
Centra Labs	East Millstone, NJ	(732) 873-2550	www.centralabs.com	Storage
Certus International, Inc.	St. Louis, MO	(636) 519-1699	www.certusintl.com	Project management, development
CharterHouse Clinical	London, England	+44 (0) 208 741 7170	www.charterhouse-clinical.com	Phase II, III, IV, validation, storage
Chiltern International	Carlsbad, CA	(760) 707-5025	www.chiltern.com	QA/QC
Cirion	Laval, Quebec	(450) 688-6445	www.cirion.ca	Project management, validation, phase II, III, IV
Clinical Data Care	Lund, Sweden	+46 46 31 32 00	www.clinicaldatacare.com	Programming
Clinical Horizons Research	Leonia, NJ	(201) 585-2470	www.chrinc.com	Phase II, monitoring, development, packaging
Clinical R&D Services	Wayne, NJ	(973) 696-0824	www.clinicalrdservices.com	Phase II, III, IV
Clinical Research Consulting, Inc.	Boston, MA	(508) 865-8907	www.eclinicalresearchconsulting.com	Project management, QA
Clinical Trial Management Services, Inc.	Bristol, TN	(800) 422-3596	Ctmsinc.com	QA

Vendor	Location	Phone #	Website	Clinical Support	Phase I Clinicals	Clinical Trial Management	Clinical Statistics	Additional Services
Clinimetrics	San Jose, CA	(408) 452-8215	www.clinimetrics.com		X	X	X	Phase II, project management, development
ClinStat, Inc.	Ontario, Canada	(613) 328-3068	www.clinstat.ca				X	Development
ClinTrust Global Alliance	Cambridgeshire, UK	(214) 630-0288	N/A			X	X	Consulting, project management, development, QA/QC
CNS	Australia	+617 3232 7026	www.clinetserv.com		X			Development
Cortrial	Berlin, Germany	+49 (30) 435 58 93 0	www.cortrial.com		X			Development
Covance	Princeton, NJ	(888) COVANCE	www.covance.com		X	X	X	Stability, clinical design & management, consulting
CPT Co.	Fairfield, NJ	(973) 808-7111	www.cptclabs.com		X			Method validation, stability, product testing
CRC	New Orleans, LA	(504) 581-1574	www.crc2000.com		X			QC/QA, phase II, III, IV
CRL	Lenexa, KS	(800) 445-6917	www.crlcorp.com		X			Development, phase II, III, IV
CroMedica	La Jolla, CA	(858) 558-3888	www.cromedica.com			X		
CTMS	Bristol, TN	(888) 422-3596	Ctmsinc.com		X			
CTSI	Elverson, PA	(800) 398-8261	www.ctsi-cro.com			X		Project management, QA
DATAMAP GmbH	Freiburg, Germany	++49 (761) 4 52 08-0	www.datamap.de				X	Validation, programming
DaVita Inc.	Minneapolis, MN	(612) 347-6367	www.davitaresearch.com		X			Phase II, III, IV
DP Clinical	Rockville, MD	(301) 294-6226	www.dpclinical.com		X			Development, QA
DPT	San Antonio, TX	(866) CALL DPT	www.dptlabs.com			X		
Dynarand	San Francisco, CA	(888) 794-IRVS	www.dynarand.com	X				
ECA	Tlalpan, Mexico	+52-55-5876-1626	www.eca.com.mx				X	Programming, project management, QA/QC
ECRON WIEDEY Research	Frankfurt am Main, Germany	+49 69 6680300	www.ecrom.com				X	
Emissary	Austin, TX	(512) 918-1992	www.sendemissary.com		X	X	X	Phase II, III, IV, QA

Company	Location	Phone	Website			Services
EPS Company, Ltd	Tokyo, Japan	+81-3-5804-7577	www.eps.co.jp		X	Programming, QA/QC, randomization
Estoerix Inc.	Calabasas, CA	(800) 586-4654	www.esoterix.com	X		Method validation, phase II, III, IV
GENTIAE Clinical Research	San Francisco, CA	(415) 715-2317	www.gentiae.com		X	Development
Global Pharma Alliance	Newport Beach, CA	(800) 311-0221	www.globalpa.com	X		Project management, development, QA
GNB Limited	UK	44 0 20 8295 1314	www.gnb.ltd.uk		X	Validation
Grayline Clinical Drug Trials	Wichita Falls, TX	(800) 782-0895	www.graylinecdt.com		X	Phase II, III, IV
Gulf Coast Research Associates, Inc.	Baton Rouge, LA	(225) 757-1084	www.gulfcoastra.com		X	Phase II, III, IV
Health Decisions	Oxford, UK	+44 1865 338005	www.healthdec.com		X	Project management
Health Research Associates, Inc.	Mountlake Terrace, WA	(425) 775-6565	www.hrainc.net		X	Consulting, project management
Hollister-Stier	Spokane, WA	(800) 992-1120	www.hollister-stier.com	X		QC, manufacturing, method development and validation
HPM Healthcare and Project Management	Geneva, Switzerland	41 22 792 40 44	www.hpmgeneva.ch		X	Phase II, III, IV
Huntingdon Life Sciences Group plc	England	+44 148-089-2000	www.huntingdon.com	X		Phase II, III
Hurley Consulting Associates, Ltd	Chatham, NJ	(973) 635-9898	www.hurleyconsulting.com		X	
ICON Clinical Research	North Wales, PA	(215) 616-3000	www.iconclinical.com	X	X	Project management, QA/QC
idv Data Analysis and Study Planning	Munich, Germany	49 89 8508001	N/A		X	Programming, development
Ilex Oncology Inc.	San Antonio, TX	(210) 949-8200	www.ilexoncology.com	X		Phase II, III
Ingenium Research, Inc.	Cary, NC	(919) 462-8867	www.ingen-inc.com		X	Validation, randomization
Integrated Research, Inc.	Quebec, Canada	(514) 683-1909	www.iricanada.com		X	Development
International Drug Development Institute	Cambridge, MA	(866) TEL-IDDI	www.iddi.com			
Inveresk Research	Scotland / Cary, NC	+44 (0) 1875 614545 / (800) 988-9845	www.inversek.com	X	X	Validation, phase II, III, IV, stability, storage, inhalation, project management
IPS	Bridgewater, NJ	(800) 644-5844	www.intl-pharm-srv.com	X		

Vendor	Location	Phone #	Website	Clinical Statistics	Clinical Trial Management	Phase I Clinicals	Clinical Support	Additional Services
Kendle Intl. Inc.	Cincinnati, OH	(513) 381-5550	www.kendle.com	X		X		Software, validation, project management
Köhler GmbH, Dr. Manfred	Freiburg, Germany	+49 761 50318 0	www.koehler-freiburg.de	X				Programming, randomization
LCG Bioscience	Cambridge, UK	+44 1954 717217	www.bioscience.com				X	Development
Leake	Richmond, VA	(800) 253-2402	www.leakeinc.com					
Lovelace Respiratory Research Institute	Albuquerque, NM	(888) 300-9080	www.lrri.org			X		Phase II, III, IV
MAJARO InfoSystems, Inc.	San Jose, CA	(408) 562-1890	www.majaro.com	X				Validation, programming, project management
Maxxam Analytics Inc.	Toronto, Canada; Calgary, Canada; Montreal, Canada; Edmonton, Canada	(905) 890-2555; (403) 291-3077; (514) 636-6218; (780) 468-3500	www.maxxam.ca	X		X		Phase II, III, IV
McKesson	Rockville, MD	(888) 4-MBS-BIO	www.mckessonbio.com		X			Phase II, III, IV, packaging
MDS	Quebec, Canada	(514) 333-0033	www.mdsps.com	X	X	X		Management
Meddoc	Denmark	45 45 76 8555	www.meddoc.com		X	X		
Medfiles	Estonia	+372 7 303 979	www.medfiles.ee			X		Phase II, III, IV, translation
MedFocus Clinical Research Consulting Opportunities	Des Plaines, IL	(800) 256-4625	www.medfocus.com	X				Programming, project management
Medical & Technical Research Associates	Natick, MA	(508) 650-0085	www.mtra.com		X			
Medichem	Woodridge, IL	(866) MEDICHEM	www.medichem.com			X		Phase II, III, IV, stability, validation, development
MediMentum ApS	Hilleroed, Denmark	+45 48 22 9410	N/A	X				Consulting, programming
Medpace LLC	Cincinnati, OH	(800) 730-5779	www.medpace.com	X	X			Programming, project management

Company	Location	Phone	Website			Services
Medtox Laboratories Inc.	St. Paul, MN	(800) 832-3244	www.medtox.com	X		Phase II, III, IV, QC, QA
Meridian Software, Inc.	Raleigh, NC	(919) 518-1070	www.meridiansoftware.com	X		Consulting, programming
MetaWorks Inc.	Medford, MA	(781) 395-0700	www.metaworksinc.com	X		Consulting
Micromedex	Greenwood Village, CO	(303) 486-6400	www.micromedex.com		X	
Midwest Research Institute	Kansas City, MO	(816) 753-7600	www.mriresearch.org	X		Method validation
Millennix Inc.	Purchase, NJ	(914) 694-4949	www.millennix-inc.com	X		Phase II, III, IV
Msource Medical Development	Kraainem, Belgium	+32-2-7683.01.66	www.msource-cro.com		X	Project management, development, QA/QC
MTRA/AAI	Natick, MA	(508) 650-0085	www.mtra.com		X	Phase II, III, IV, stability, validation, development
New Drug Services, Inc.	Kennett Square, PA	(610) 444-4722	www.newdrugservice.com	X	X	Programming, project management, development, pharmacokinetics/ pharmacodynamic modeling & analysis, phase II, III, IV
NOCCR	New Orleans, LA	(504) 826-5000	www.noccr.com	X		Phase II, III, IV
North Coast Clinical Lab	Sandusky, OH	(419) 626-6012	www.northcoastlab.com	X		QC
Northwest Kinetics, L.L.C.	Tacoma, WA	(253) 593-5304	www.nwkinetics.com	X		Phase I, II, pharmacokinetics, QA
Nth Analytics	Princeton, NJ	(908) 672-5649	www.nthanalytics.com		X	Validation, programming
Nucro Technics	Scarborough, Ontario	(416) 438-6727	www.nucro.com	X		Phase II, III, IV, method validation
Omnicare	King of Prussia, PA	(800) 290-5766	www.omnicarecr.com		X	Storage, packaging, project management, QA
Operatix Consulting Inc.	Waterdown, Ontario	(905) 690-1200	www.operatrix.com		X	Project management
P3 Research, Ltd	Wellington, New Zealand	64 49 14 4640	www.p3research.co.nz		X	
Pacific Data Designs, Inc.	San Francisco, CA	(415) 776-0660	Home.pdd.net		X	QA
Paragon	Irvine, CA	(949) 224-2800	www.parabio.com	X		Programming, project management, QA/QC
PAREXEL Intl. Corp.	Boston, MA	(781) 487-9900	www.parexel.com	X		Phase II, III, IV, validation
Patheon	Mississauga, Ontario	(888) 728-4366	www.patheon.com	X		Development, packaging
PeachTree Clinical Research	Atlanta, GA	(770) 716-9450	peachtreeclinicalresearch.com	X	X	
Pharma Medica	Ontario, Canada	(905) 624-9115 (877) PHARMA1	www.pharmamedica.com	X	X	Phase II, III, IV, development, validation

Vendor	Location	Phone #	Website	Clinical Support	Phase I Clinicals	Clinical Trial Management	Clinical Statistics	Additional Services
Pharmaceutical Consultants, Inc.	Leawood, KS	(913) 491-9825	www.pharmconsult.com			X		Verification, development
Pharmaceutical Profiles	Princeton, NJ	(609) 951-2205	www.pharmprofiles.com		X			
Pharmaceutical Service Network	Eindhoven, The Netherlands	+31 40 243 3070	www.psn-europe.com				X	Project management
Pharmadata	Marietta, GA	(770) 579-8812	www.pharmdata.com		X			Project management, QA
PharmaKinetics Laboratories Inc.	Baltimore, MD	(410) 385-4500	www.pharmakinetics.com		X			Phase III, IV
PharmaLinkFHI	RTP, NC	(919) 484-1921	www.pharmalinkfhi.com				X	Project management, development
Pharmanet	Princeton, NJ	(609) 951-6800	www.pharmanet.com			X		QC/QA, project management, consulting
PharmaPart	Thalwil, Switzerland	41 (0) 1 723 59 59	www.pharmapart.com				X	Consulting, project management, QA/QC
PharmData, Inc.	Marietta, GA	(770) 579-8812	www.pharmdata.com				X	Programming, project management, development
Phase Forward	Waltham, MA	(888) 703-1122	www.phaseforward.com			X		Consulting
Phase I	Santa Fe, NM	(505) 471-8438	www.phase1tox.com	X	X			
Physicians Mgt. Systems for Clinical Research, Inc.	Bakersfield, CA	(877) 588-7418	www.pmscr.com	X		X		QA
PPD, Inc.	Austin, TX	(512) 5819156	www.ppdi.com	X	X			QA, QC, pharmacokinetics
PRA International	McLean, VA	(703) 748-0760	www.prainternational.com	X	X	X		Phase II, QA, project management
PRACS	Fargo, ND	(701) 239-4750	www.pracs.com	X	X			
PROLOGUE RESEARCH	Columbus, OH	(614) 324-1500	www.procro.com					Programming, project management, development
PSI	Saint Petersburg, Moscow, Kiev, Sofia, Bucharest	+32 2 675 4890	www.psi.ru				X	Phase I, II, III, development, consulting

Company	Location	Phone	Website			Services
Psychiatric Research Institute	Wichita, KA	(316) 291-4774	www.pri-research.org	X		Phase I, II, III
QTI	Whitehouse, NJ	(908) 534-4455	www.QTIonline.com		X	Method development, stability
RCC	Switzerland	+41 61 975 11 11	www.rcc.ch	X		Inhalation, phase II, III
Red River Statistics, Inc.	Shreveport, LA	(318) 868-0720	Home.earthlink.net/~rrstat/		X	SAS
Research Dynamics Consulting Group, Ltd	Pittsford, NY	(585) 381-1350	www.resdyncg.com		X	Consulting, monitoring
Rho, Inc.	Chapel Hill, NC	(919) 408-8000	www.rhoworld.com		X	Programming, randomization
Rohrbaugh Associates, Inc.	Newtown, PA	(215) 598-8400	N/A		X	Project management
RPS	Plymouth Meeting, PA	(866) RPS-1151	www.rpsweb.com		X	Programming, project management, QA/QC
Scandinavian CRI AB	Göteborg, Sweden	+46 31 703 18 50	www.scandinavianccri.se		X	Development
Schiff and Co.	West Caldwell, NJ	(973) 227-1830	www.schiffco.com		X	Development, phase II, III, IV
SciAn Research Services	Toronto, Canada	(416) 231-8008	www.scian.com		X	Consulting
Scirex Corporation	Horsham, PA	(215) 646-4117	www.scirex.com	X		Consulting
Sequani	UK	+44 (0) 1531 634121	www.sequani.com	X		QA, management
SGS Biopharma	Wavre, Belgium	+32 10 421 111	www.sgsbiopharma.com		X	QA/QC
Simbec	UK	+44 1443 690977	www.simbec.co.uk	X		Phase II, III, QA
Smith Hanley Consulting Group	Lake Mary, FL	(800) 684-9921	www.smithhanley-consulting.com		X	Programming, project management
SMO-USA, Inc.	Conyers, GA	(770) 785-7745	www.smo-usa.com		X	Phase II, III, IV
Solutia	St. Louis, MO	(314) 674-1000	www.psd-solutia.com	X		
Southern Research Institute	Birmingham, AL	(888) 322-1166 (205) 322-7472	www.southernresearch.com	X		Cancer, phase II, III
Spadille	Denmark	45 48 48 41 00	www.spadille.com		X	QA
Statisticians WithOut Borders	Bahama, NC	(919) 477-4007	www.statisticinaswithoutborders.com		X	Programming
STATKING Consulting Inc.	Fairfield, OH	(513) 858-2989	www.statkingconsulting.com		X	Programming, development, randomization
STATPROBE, Inc.	Ann Arbor, MI	(734) 769-5000	www.statprobe.com		X	Programming, project management
Stat-Trade, Inc.	Morrisville, PA	(215) 428-9680	www.stattrade.com		X	Programming
Symbiance, Inc.	Princeton, NJ	(609) 243-9050	www.symbiance.com		X	Programming, project management, development
SyMetric Sciences	Quebec, Canada	(514) 935-4562	www.symetric.ca	X		Project management, randomization
SYMFO	Cambridge, MA	(866) 88-SYMFO	www.symfo.com			

Vendor	Location	Phone #	Website	Clinical Support	Phase I Clinicals	Clinical Trial Management	Clinical Statistics	Additional Services
Synergos, Inc.	The Woodlands, TX	(281) 367-665	www.synergosinc.com		X	X	X	Phase II, III, IV, development
Synteract, Inc.	Encinitas, CA	(760) 634-2133	www.synteract.com		X	X	X	Programming, project management, development, randomization
Target Health Inc.	New York, NY	(212) 681-2100	www.targethealth.com			X	X	
TERRE Clinical Research Services, Inc.	Ann Arbor, MI	(734) 663-9030	www.terrecrs.com			X		
TNO BIBRA	UK	+44 (0) 20 8652 1040	www.tnobibra.com		X			Phase II
Trial Management Group, Inc.	Toronto, Canada		www.tmginvestigators.com			X		Phase II, III, IV
Triphasic Clinical Trials Laboratories	UK	+44 0 1752 777771	www.triphasic.co.uk	X				
U. of Iowa Div. of Pharm. Science	Iowa City, IA	(319) 335-8674	www.uiowa.edu/~pharmaser		X			Method
		(319) 335-4096	www.uiowa.edu/~cadd					validation
Uppsala Monitoring Centre	Uppsala, Sweden	+46 1865 6060	www.who-umc.org				X	
Viridae Clinical Sciences Inc.	Vancouver, Canada	(604) 689-9404	www.viridae.com		X			Phase II, III, IV
Virtu Stat, Ltd	North Wales, PA	(215) 699-2424	www.virtustat.com				X	Validation, programming, randomization
VPDC, Inc.	Chicago, IL	(773) 286-4301	www.vpdc.com			X		
West Pharmaceutical Service	Lionville, PA	(610) 594-2900	www.westpharma.com		X			Device & package components, drug-package, interactions
WinPharm Associates, LLC	San Francisco, CA	(925) 244-9820	www.winpharm-associates.com			X		Packaging, distribution
YRCR	Oxon, UK	44 14 91 410866	www.xrcr.com			X		

Regulatory Services

Vendor	Location	Phone #	Website	IND Preparation	NDA Preparation	Annual update Preparation	Regulatory advisors	Additional Services
Advanced Biologics	Lambertville, NJ	(609) 397-7891	www.advbiol.com	X			X	Programming, vaccine
Advanced Clinical Services	Schaumbrug, IL	(847) 995-9222	www.advancedclinical.com	X		X	X	QA, SAS
Advanced Research Corporation	St. Petersburg, FL	(727) 897-9095	www.arc-cro.com	X		X		QA
Agallaco and Associates	Belle Mead, NJ	(908) 874-7558	Agallaco.com		X			Validation, manufacturing
Algorithm Pharma Inc.	Laval, Quebec	(514) 858-6077	www.algopharm.com	X			X	QA/QC, development
Allied Clinical Research	Ontario, Canada	(905) 238 0599	www.allied-research.com	X				Phase II, III, method development
AON	Chicago, IL	312.381.1000	www.aon.com			X	X	Development
Applied Logic Associates, Inc.	Houston, TX	(713) 583-4747	www.alogic.com		X	X	X	Development
ArisGlobal, LLC	Stamford, CT	(203) 588-3000	www.arisglobal.com	X	X		X	Project management
Arkios Bio Development International	Virginia Beach, VA	(757) 228-3255	www.arkios.com	X	X		X	Project management
Barton and Plansky Associates, Inc.	New York, NY	(212) 688-4343	www.bpa-mcs.com				X	QA/QC
Beardsworth Consulting Group, Inc.	Flemington, NJ	(908) 788-1729	www.beardsworth.com	X	X			PLA prep, project management
Beckloff Associates, Inc.	Overland Park, KS	(913) 451-3955	www.beckloff.com	X	X	X	X	Development
Biedenbach & Stein, Inc.	Cincinnati, OH	(877) 985-9707	www.fdameetings.com			X	X	Consulting
BioCor	Yardley, PA	(215) 321-9876	www.biocor.com	X	X	X	X	Development, consulting
Brand Institute, Inc.	Miami, FL	(305) 374-2500	www.brandinstitute.com	X	X	X	X	Consulting, validation
Cambridge Regulatory Services Limited	Cambridgeshire, UK	+44 (0) 1480 465755	www.cambreg.co.uk				X	
CanReg Inc.	Dundas, Ontario	(866) 7CANREG	www.canreg.ca	X	X	X	X	Consulting, PLA prep
CCS Associates	Mountain View, CA	(650) 691-4400	www.ccsainc.com	X	X			QA
Celeris Corporation	Nashville, TN	(615) 341-0223	www.celeriscorp.com				X	BLA prep, PLA prep
Certus International, Inc.	St. Louis, MO	(636) 519-1699	www.certusintl.com		X		X	Development, project management
ClinForce, Inc.	Durham, NC	(800) 964-2877	www.clinforce.com				X	Programming, project management

Company	Location	Phone	Website	Services
Clinical Data Care	Lund, Sweden	+46 46 31 32 00	www.clinicaldatacare.com	Programming
COVALENT GROUP, INC.	Wayne, PA	(610) 975-9533	www.covalentgroup.com	Development, project management, randomization
Covance Inc.	Princeton, NJ	(888) COVANCE	www.covance.com	Consulting
CTSI	Elverson, PA	(800) 398-8261	www.ctsi-cro.com	QA, project management
DataCeutics, Inc.	Pottstown, PA	(610) 970-2333	www.dataceutics.com	Validation, consulting, project management
Dataform, Inc.	Marlborough, MA	(508) 624-6454	www.datafarminc.com	Consulting, PLA prep
ECA	Tlalpan, Mexico	+52 55 5876 1626	www.eca.com.mx	Programming, project management, QA/QC
Emissary Inc.	Austin, TX	(512) 918-1992	www.sendemissary.com	Development, project management
EMMES Corporation	Rockville, MD	(301) 251-1161	www.emmes.com	QC, project management
eResearch Technology	Philadelphia, PA	(215) 972-0420	www.ert.com	
Evolving Technologies Corporation			www.evolvingtech.com	QA, CANDA
EZ Associates	Berkeley Heights, NJ	(908) 464-4423	www.ezassociates.com	Development
First Consulting Group	Wayne, PA	(866) 287-3792	www.lifesciences.fcg.com	Consulting
God Consulting Services	Cary, NC	(919) 233-2926	www.gadconsulting.com	Consulting
Galt Associates, Inc.	Sterling, VA	(703) 433-6106	www.DrugSafety.com	Consulting
Health Decisions	Oxford, UK	+44 1865 338005	www.healthdec.com	Project management
Hurd & Associates, Inc.	Evanston, IL	(847) 864-9773	N/A	QA/QC, consulting, BLA prep
Icagen, Inc.	Durham, NC / RTP, NC	(919) 941-5206	www.icagen.com	
ICON Clinical Research	North Wales, PA	(215) 616-3000	www.iconclinical.com	QA/QC, project management
IDRAC	Fort Washington, PA	(215) 619-6000	www.idrac.com	
Image Solutions, Inc.	Morristown, NJ	(973) 292-6444	www.imagesolutions.com	BLA prep, consulting
IMIC	Colonia Roma Mexico, Mexico	(800) 292-8849	www.imicresearch.com	QA/QC
INC Research	Raleigh, NC	(919) 876-9300	www.incresearch.com	Project management, development
Ingenium Research, Inc.	Cary, NC	(919) 462-8867	www.ingen-inc.com	Validation, randomization
Integrated Research Inc.	Montreal, Quebec	(514) 683-1909	www.iricanada.com	Development
Inveresk Research	Cary, NC	(800) 988-9845	www.inveresk.com	Project management
Irwin G. Martin, PhD	Ann Arbor, MI	734-649-5605	www.irwin-martin.com	
Jarosz Regulatory Services, Inc.	Whitewater, WI	(262) 473-4255	www.jrsweb.com	CTX prep
Kendle International	Cincinnati, OH	(513) 381 5550	www.kendle.com	Phase II, III, IV
KROSS, Inc.	Hillsborough, NJ	(908) 369-1900	www.kross-inc.com	Validation, QA/QC, stability

Vendor	Location	Phone #	Website	IND Preparation	NDA Preparation	Annual update Preparation	Regulatory advisors	Additional Services
Kruse Consulting Group	Cheyenne, WY / Burlington, VT / Haddonfield, NJ	(307) 634-7697 / (802) 899-3473 / (856) 428-6374	www.kruseconsultinggroup.com	X	X		X	QA, project management
Lineberry Research Associates	RTP, NC	(919) 547-0970	www.lineberryresearch.com	X	X			Development, IB
Liquent Inc.	Fort Washington, PA	(215) 619-6000	www.liquent.com	X	X	X	X	BLA prep, consulting
Lorenz Hoffman	Chapel Hill, NC	(919) 918-7707	lorenzhofmann.com	X	X			
Magellan Labs	RTP, NC / Somerset, NJ / San Diego, CA	(919) 481-4855 / (732) 302-1400 / (858) 547-7800	www.magellanlabs.com	X	X			Stability, validation
MAJARO InfoSystems, Inc.	Albuquerque, NM / San Jose, CA	(815) 338-9500 / (408) 562-1890	www.majaro.com	X	X		X	Validation, project management
McCarthy Consultant Services, Inc.	Newmarket, Ontario	(905) 836-0033	www.mccarthyconsultant.com	X	X	X	X	Consulting, QA/QC
Med Exec International	Glendale, CA	(800) 507-5277	www.medexcintl.com				X	QA/QC
MedFocus Clinical Research Consulting Opportunities	Des Plaines, IL	(800) 256-4625	www.medfocus.com		X			Consulting, project management
Medichem	Woodridge, IL	(630) 783-4600	www.medichem.com	X	X			Development, scale up
Mediscience Planning, Inc.	Tokyo, Japan	03-3663-7575	www.mpi-cro.co.jp	X	X			Stability, phase II, III
MEDISCRIBE, INC.	Cary, NC	(919) 468-8518	www.mediscribe.com	X	X		X	IB, development
Medpace LLC	Cincinnati, OH	(513) 579-9911	www.medpace.com		X		X	Project management, programming
MedSource Consulting, Inc.	Houston, TX	(281) 286-2003	www.medsourceconsulting.com	X			X	Project management
MMRI	Baltimore, MD	(410) 435-4200	www.mmri.org	X	X		X	Project management
MORIAH Consultants	Yorba Linda, CA	(714) 970-0790	www.moriahconsultants.com	X	X	X	X	BLA prep, consulting
New Drug Services	Kennett Square, PA	(610) 444-4722	www.newdrugservices.com	X	X		X	QA

Company	Location	Phone	Website				Services
Nucro-Technics Inc.	Scarborough, Ontario	(416) 438-6727	www.nucro-technics.com			X	QA/QC, stability
NuGenesis Technologies Corporation	Westborough, MA	(508) 616-9876	www.nugenesis.com			X	Validation, project management, QA/QC
Octagon Research Solutions, Inc.	Plymouth Meeting, PA	(610) 825-0825	www.octagonresearch.com	X		X	Programming, QA/QC
Omnicare Clinical Research	King of Prussia, PA	(800) 856-2556	www.omnicarecr.com			X	Project management
ORA Clinical Research and Development	North Andover, MA	(978) 685-8900	www.oraclinical.com			X	Project management
Paragon	Irvine, CA	(949) 224-2800	www.parabio.com			X	Programming, project management, QA/QC
PAREXEL International Corporation	Waltham, MA	(781) 487-9900	www.parexel.com		X	X	Consulting
Pharmaceutical Regulatory Services, Inc.	Princeton, NJ	(609) 497-9694	www.pharmregservices.com		X	X	Consulting
Pharmaceutical Service Network	Eindhoven, The Netherlands	+31 40 243 3070	www.psn-europe.com			X	Project management
PharmaNet	Princeton, NJ	(609) 951-6800	www.pharmanet-cro.com			X	Consulting
PharmaPart	Thalwil, Switzerland	+41 (0) 1 723 59 59	www.pharmapart.com		X	X	Consulting, project management, QA/QC
PharmaResearch Corporation	Wilmington, NC	(866) Pharma-1	www.pharmaresearch.com			X	QA/QC
PharmData, Inc.	Marietta, GA	(770) 879-8812	www.pharmdata.com	X			Programming, project management, development
Phoenix Regulatory Associates, Ltd	Sterling, VA	(703) 406-0906	www.phoenixrising.com	X		X	Validation
Pipeline Development Solutions, Inc.	Lebanon, PA	(717) 273.9568	www.pipelineds.com	X		X	QA, project management
PPD Development	Morrisville, NC	(919) 462-5600	www.ppddiscovery.com	X	X	X	Project management
PPD Discovery	Wilmington, NC	(910) 251-0081	www.ppddevelopment.com	X	X		Project management
PRA International	McLean, VA	(703) 748-0760	www.prainternational.com	X		X	
Precision Research, Inc.	Malvern, PA	(610) 296-1744	www.precise.net	X			
ProSeed Biotech Services, Inc.	Boston, MA	(617) 227-5647	www.proseedcapital.com/biotech	X			IB, project management, development
PSI International, Inc.	Fairfax, VA	(703) 352-9482	www.psiint.com		X	X	Consulting
RCN Associates, Inc.	Annapolis, MD	(410) 263-3355	www.rcnrx.com	X			
Recruitech International, Inc.	Glenside, PA	(215) 576-7400	www.recruitech.com			X	Project management, QA/QC

Vendor	Location	Phone #	Website	IND Preparation	NDA Preparation	Annual update Preparation	Regulatory advisors	Additional Services
Regulatory Affairs, North America LLC	Durham, NC	(919) 479-9956	www.ranallc.com	X		X	X	Consulting, CTX prep, IB
Regulatory/Clinical Consultants, Inc.	Lee's Summit, MO	(816) 347-9224	www.rxcci.com		X	X	X	QA/QC
Rohrbaugh Associates, Inc.	Newtown, PA	(215) 598-8400	www.rohrbaughassociates.com	X	X			Project management
RPS	Plymouth Meeting, PA	(866) RPS-1151	www.rpsweb.com				X	Programming, project management, QA/QC
Schiff & Company	West Caldwell, NJ	(973) 277-1830	www.schiffco.com				X	
Simbec Research Limited	South Wales, UK	+44 (0) 1443 690977	www.simbec.co.uk				X	Project management
Smith Hanley Consulting Group	Lake Mary, FL	(407) 805-3010	www.smithhanley-consulting.com		X			Programming, project management
SRI	Menlo Park, CA	(650) 859-2000	www.sri.com	X				QA, pharmacokinetics
Statisticians WithOut Borders	Bahama, NC	(919) 477-4007	www.statisticianswithoutborders.com		X			Programming
Stat-Trade, Inc.	Morrisville, PA	(215) 428-9680	www.stattrade.com	X			X	Programming
Synarc, Inc.	Maynard, MA	(781) 685-2700	www.synarc.com		X		X	Project management, development
Target Health Inc.	New York, NY	(212) 681-2100	www.targethealth.com	X			X	QA, project management
TherImmune	Gaithersburg, MD	(301) 330-3733	www.therimmune.com	X			X	
TRI	Bethesda, MD	(301) 564-6400	www.tech-res-intl.com	X				
Trilliant Research Inc.	Marlton, NJ	(856) 793-0484	www.trilliantresearch.com	X	X		X	Project management, development
TriPharmSafety, Inc.	Raleigh, NC	(919) 870-5772	drugsafety.home.mindspring.com	X	X			Project management
VA Cooperative Studies Program	Albuquerque, NM	(505) 248-3203	www.va.gov/resdev	X				Packaging, randomization
Wainwright Associates Ltd	Berkshire, UK	+44 (0) 1628 670355	www.wainwrightassociates.co.uk			X	X	Consulting, CTX prep
Weissinger Solutions, Inc.	Saratoga, CA	(408) 741-8131	www.weissinger.com	X	X	X	X	BLA prep, consulting, IB

Contract Laboratory
Audit Check List

Audit#:_____ Date:_____ Auditor:_____

1. Study Title: _____

2. Laboratory: _____

3. Address: _____

4. Date of Audit: _____

5. Auditor: _____

6. Date of Last FDA Inspection of Laboratory: _____

7. Date of Last CarboMedics Audit of Laboratory: _____

8. Facility Manager: _____

9. Study Director: _____

10. Quality Assurance Unit: _____

	Unaccept	Needs Imp.	Accept	Excellent
11. **Protocol:**				
a. Title and Purpose of Study				
b. Identification of Test and Control Articles				
c. Name of Sponsor and Name and Address of Testing Facility				
d. Description of Animal Model				
e. Rationale for Animal Model				
f. Procedure for Identification of Test System				
g. Description of Experimental Design				
h. Description of Animal Diet				
i. Administration of Test or Control Article				
j. Type and Frequency of Tests, Analyses, and Measurements				
k. Records to be Maintained				
l. Date of Approval and Dated Signature of Study Director				
m. Statistical Methods to be Used				
n. Changes (with Reasons) Approved and Maintained with Protocol				
12. Master Schedule Sheet (Test system, Nature of Study, Date Study was Initiated, Current Status, Identity of Sponsor, and Name of Study Director)				

	Unaccept	Needs Imp.	Accept	Excellent
13. Current Summary of Training and Experience and Job Description for Each Individual				
14. Personnel Qualifications				
15. **Quality Assurance (QA) Unit:**				
a. Independent of Personnel Engaged in Study				
b. Written Procedure for Operation of QA Unit				
c. Maintains Copy of Master Schedule Sheet				
d. Maintains Copy of All Protocols				
e. Inspections at Intervals Adequate to Assure Integrity				
f. Written Reports of Periodic Inspections				
g. Significant Problems Reported to Study Director and Management				
h. Written Status Reports on Each Study				
i. Reviews Final Study Report				
j. All QA Unit Records are Kept in One Location				
16. **Written Procedures:**				
a. Animal Care				
b. Animal Care Facilities				
c. Animal Transfer and Identification				
d. Characterization of Test and Control Articles				
e. Handling of Test and Control Articles				
f. Methods of Synthesis, Fabrication, or Derivation of Test and Control Articles				
g. Determination of Stability of Test and Control Articles				
h. Determination of Stability of Carrier Mixtures				
i. Test System Observations				
j. Laboratory Testing				
k. Handling of Moribund or Dead				
l. Necropsy or Postmortem Examination of Animals				
m. Collection and Identification of Specimens				
n. Histopathology				
o. Inspection, Cleaning, Maintenance, Testing, Calibration, and Standardization of Equipment				
p. Data Handling and Storage				
17. Testing Facilities of Suitable Size and Construction				
18. Spaces for Cleaning, Sterilizing, and Maintaining Equipment and Supplies				
19. **Equipment:**				
a. Adequate Equipment Including Environmental Control Equipment				
b. Equipment Cleanliness				
c. Adherence to Cleaning, Maintenance, Calibration, and Standardization Schedules				

			Unaccept	Needs Imp.	Accept	Excellent
	d.	Records of All Inspection, Maintenance, Testing, Calibration, and Standardization Operations				
	e.	Records Include Defects, How and When Defects were Found, and Remedial Action				
20.		Labeling of Reagents and Solutions (Identity, Titer or Concentration, Storage Requirements, and Expiration Date)				
21.		**Test and Control Articles:**				
	a.	Records of Identity, Strength, Purity, and Composition of Each Batch				
	b.	Stability Determined				
	c.	Records of Stability Testing				
	d.	Labeling of Storage Containers				
	e.	Storage				
	f.	Retention of Reserve Samples				
	g.	Handling				
	h.	Testing of Carrier Mixtures				
	i.	Records of Stability Testing of Carrier Mixtures				
	j.	Labeling of Carrier Mixtures				
22.		**Animal Facilities:**				
	a.	Sufficient Number of Animal Rooms and Areas:				
		(1) Separation of Species and Test Systems				
		(2) Isolation of Individual Projects				
		(3) Isolation of Newly Received Animals				
		(4) Routine and Specialized Housing of Animals				
		(5) Isolation of Studies Using Biohazardous Materials				
		(6) Separate Areas, as appropriate, for Diagnosis, Treatment, and Control of Animal Diseases				
	b.	Facilities for Collection and Disposal of Animal Waste and Refuse				
	c.	Storage Areas for Feed, Bedding, Supplies, and Equipment				
	d.	Areas for Handling Test and Control Articles				
	e.	Space for Aseptic Surgery, Intensive Care, Necropsy, Histology, Radiography, and Handling of Biohazardous Materials				
23.		**Animal Care:**				
	a.	Isolation of Newly Received Animals				
	b.	Animals Free of Any Disease or Condition that Could Interfere with Study				
	c.	Records or Diagnosis and Treatment of Animal Disease				
	d.	Animal Identification				
	e.	Separation of Different Species				
	f.	Cleaning of Cages and Equipment				
	g.	Records of Periodic Analyses of Feed and Water				
	h.	Bedding Does Not Interfere with Study Purpose or Conduct				
	i.	Records of Use of Pest Control Materials				

		Unaccept	Needs Imp.	Accept	Excellent
j.	Pest Control Materials Do Not Interfere with Study				
24.	Identification of Specimens (Test System, Study, Nature, and Date of Collection)				
25.	Records Available to Pathologists when Examining Specimens Histopathologically				
26.	Records of All Deviations from Written Procedures, Including Authorization				
27.	All Records Specified in Protocol are Maintained				
28.	Data Entries (Manual and Computer)				
29.	Availability of Laboratory Manuals and Written Procedures				
30.	Study Conducted in Accordance with Protocol				
31.	Test Systems Monitored in Conformity with Protocol				
32.	Personnel Report Adverse Health or Medical Condition				
33.	Final Study Reports Include (as a Minimum) Name and Address of Facility Performing Study, Start and Completion Dates of Study, Objectives and Procedures Stated in the Protocol, Changes to Protocol, Statistical Methods for Data Analysis, Test and Control Articles Used, Stability of Test and Control Articles, Methods Used, Test System Used, Dosage and its Administration, All Circumstances That Could Have Affected the Data, Names of Key Members of Study Team, Operations Performed on the Data, Summary and Analysis of Data, Conclusions Drawn, Signed and Dated Reports of Key Members of Study Team, Data and Specimen Storage Locations, Statement Prepared and Signed by QA Unit, Dated Signature of Study Director, and Corrections and Additions (in the Form of Amendments) to Final Study Reports				
34.	Data Handling and Storage:				
a.	Retention of All Raw Data, Documentation, Protocols, Required Specimens, and Final Study Reports				
b.	Archives Orderly and Minimize Deterioration of Documents and Specimens				
c.	An Individual is Responsible for Archives				
d.	Index of Material in Archives				
e.	Historical File of all Obsolete Documents				
f.	Retention Period of at Least 2 Years from Date of Approval by FDA of a Research or Marketing Permit or from Study Termination Date for Studies that are not included in an FDA Submission, Except at Least 5 Years from Date of Submittal to FDA if in Support of an IND or IDE				

35. Comments:_____

_____

_____

_____

_____

_____

_____

36. Auditor's Signature:_____   37. Date:_____

cc: _____

_____

_____

References: Singer, D.C.; Upton, Ronald P.; *Guidelines for Quality Auditing*; ASQC Quality Press, 1993
Robert E. Spinock Consultants; Sample Audit Checklist, 1988

Audit Coordinator Approval:

_____   _____
Audit Coordinator   Date

Index

9 780415 299039

For Product Safety Concerns and Information please contact our EU
representative GPSR@taylorandfrancis.com
Taylor & Francis Verlag GmbH, Kaufingerstraße 24, 80331 München, Germany

www.ingramcontent.com/pod-product-compliance
Ingram Content Group UK Ltd.
Pitfield, Milton Keynes, MK11 3LW, UK
UKHW021827240425
457818UK00006B/106